Cheryl's Poems

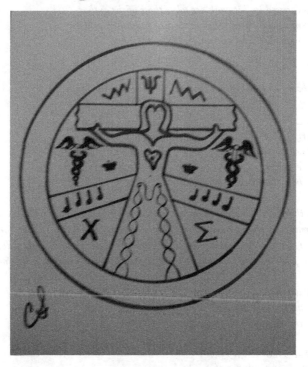

Cheryl Swofford

CHERYL'S POEMS

iUniverse books may be ordered through booksellers or by contacting:

iUniverse
1663 Liberty Drive
Bloomington, IN 47403
www.iuniverse.com
1-800-Authors (1-800-288-4677)

ISBN: 978-1-5320-4293-5 (sc)
ISBN: 978-1-5320-4295-9 (hc)
ISBN: 978-1-5320-4294-2 (e)

Library of Congress Control Number: 2018902194

Print information available on the last page.

iUniverse rev. date: 02/27/2018

Contents

——◈✦◈——

Ecstasy Amid the Storm

Ecstasy found amid the storm;
Grasping brief respite in a troubled sea;
Clinging to each other through the night;
Floundering by day, unknowing, afraid;
Tossed between pleasure and pain;
The storm all around,
Its winds tearing and separating;
Too strong, brewing before our birth;
Carrying you away
Where I hoped you, if not me,
Would find a calm breeze
Blowing upon you,
Making you feel good and safe.

The storm intensified, destroying, almost killing;
But can most things be rebuilt stronger than before?
Left alone to face the storm, afraid, hardly holding on;
At times, almost succumbing, seeking shelter.

Rebuilding, with hope to become stronger, better, wiser
For you, sons, daughters, self;
Wanting to live the fullest, to experience it all;
Relishing some memories, grateful for them, tormented still.

Realizing my heart, mind, body, and soul will be adrift
Until they reach yours where we both belong some day;
Recognizing too much to you to stay on one island;
Remembering the ecstasy that was, and could someday be;
Even stronger for having endured the storm.

Hearts on Fire

Hearts on fire with desire;
Souls aflame; no one to blame.
Come to me and light my fire;
Free me now and soothe my soul.

Two souls apart but not for long;
Come to me and let's go home.
Home to me is where you'll be;
Across the way, across the sea.

I see you ever in my dreams;
When I'm awake, when I'm asleep.
When we are near or we're apart;
I think of you; I feel your heart.

My heart is full of love for you;
When you are gone I'm always true.
My love for you is strong and real;
I'm more alive with love I feel.

Fill me up and feed my fire;
Lay me down and take me higher.
It's nature's plan to have desire;
I long for love, let's use our minds.

Our minds can tell us wrong from right;
My senses scream both day and night.
My silent screams cannot be heard;
Let's hear our words and do not hurt.

Hearts on fire with desire;
Souls aflame, no one to blame.
Come to me and light my fire;
Free me now and soothe my soul.

To An Infatuation

Kind and one of a kind
Capable and caring, a rare find
Catholic, please not diabolic
Kinetic, sometimes frenetic
Clinical and ethereal
Earthy and immaterial
Hearing silent crying
Instincts not lying
Concerned while hearing
Courageous while fearing
Crosses we're bearing
Feelings we're sharing
Compassionate, I know
Passionate, I imagine so
Christian characteristic
Humble, selfless, analytic
Instant recognition, constant chemistry
(I kept out a line; you can guess why)
Friend of Christ and Christ-less
Catharsis by your kindness
Consistent and comforting
Confusing and tormenting
Subtle charisma, heavenly host
Someone I admire the most
Round and round the carousel
Trying to avoid Hell
Colorless clothes on a kaleidoscope
Karyokinesis through a microscope
Acutely fun, chronically serious
Do we have the nerve
To risk getting what we deserve?
Might be better or worse in the short run
Or better or worse in the long run

Sometimes in dreams of unconscious
I'm conscious you're conscientious
Committed to kids and others
Conscience, church, and culture
Controlled by canons and commandments
Rites and rules and sacraments
Compromising converter
Love one another
Courteous and captivating
Energetic and palpitating
Celestial and worldly
Curious in the laboratory
Thinking of the past
The present going so fast
Considering the future
It hardly seems there
Karma? Strong forces
Much class, many courses
Teaching more than others teach
Reaching where others don't reach
With heart and soul and psyche
What about you and me?
Knowing more than others know
How far will our relationship go?
A gift for conceptualizing
Wondering what you're realizing
And if you dream all I'm desiring
Calming, disturbing, contained
How long will we be refrained?
Will we or won't we ever sin?
And if we do will we again?
Potentially cataclysmic
Maddening, mystical, and realistic.

Liz Taylor and Me

—◦~⊙x⊙~◦—

Last night I was thinking of star-crossed lovers;
How some lovers are helped and some hurt by others;
Like in long ago Egypt, Antony and Cleopatra,
Thus, Elizabeth Taylor and Richard Burton.
Then I realized something somewhat strange:
Four of my five former lovers had the same first name
(Michael/Mike, Larry, Richard, John)
As all but two of Elizabeth Taylor's seven husbands;
One was Debbie Reynolds' daughter Carrie Fisher's father Eddie;
I have a brother named Eddie and a niece named Debbie;
Her other husband was Conrad "Nicky" Hilton;
Conrad is the name of another niece's husband;
Nicky is the name of the wife of my nephew;
And don't even begin to think that I'm through;
Liz's son has the same name as my nephew Chris;
(I know this poem has gotten ridiculous);
And as if that's not enough coincidence,
My other former lover's middle name is Glenn;
Elizabeth Taylor's father's middle name is Lenn!

June 10

A small June wedding
More than fifty years ago today.
I was eighteen, he was nineteen,
In love and in lust, one might say.
A Friday night, my small church with our mothers,
A brother, a sister, the preacher, a few others;
Nothing fancy or expensive;
He dressed up; I made my own dress;
White satin and brocade, my veil made of net.
I was seven, he was eight, when we first met.
My sister had married his uncle, a Marine,
When she was sixteen and he was nineteen.
We vowed as do most 'til death do us part;
Didn't imagine a change of heart.
Daddy, not a fount of wisdom,
Doubted us two, not a clear reason.
I was bookish but thought I was in luck;
Don't think he'd ever read a whole book.
Couldn't take my hands off handsome him,
Although I think we were both virgins.

We would go on to have two children;
Even more love than I could ever imagine;
Our pride and joy, with his big brown eyes.
It was "I love you" at all our good-byes,
And throughout the days with lots of love;
Never dreaming someday what I could not prove.
But things stopped being what they had been,
And I never had him in my bed again.
Daddy said he'd never been so disappointed in his life*
That I no longer wanted to be a wife.

After my love for my husband was over
I took up with another lover.
It wasn't love at first sight, for I dared not dream
That someone would want me with my low self-esteem.
But my teeth were now straight, and I wasn't so skinny;
I would even soon dare to wear my first bikini.
Mother said never bring my lover to their house;
This man who wrote of the warmth of a house.
Yet one of my brothers had four ex-wives;
All welcomed by Mother with their past lives.
One with "Hell's Angel" tattooed on her shoulder.
But different standards for my parents' own daughter.

My lover wooed and wrote; we loved and laughed.
My eloquent lover longed and lured and then he left;
Then called and said, "It's like a wonderful dream
That we'll soon get to be together again."
But he got on with his life and soon got a wife.
He was brilliant and fun; I' m still bereft.
Even Anna Karenina had the help of her brother
When she lost her son after taking a lover;
And he didn't condemn her, not Oblonsky,
After Anna took up with Count Vronsky.
Like Anna, I too, thought of a train
Or a truck or a bridge to stop the pain;
Or jumping off a mountain in nearby hills;
But all I did was take fifty-some pills.
All at once and once again,
Trying once more to end the pain.
Once I took the pills and lay in the bath to drown;
Must have walked in my sleep for on my bed I was found.
Once I washed the pills down with straight alcohol,
Which I vomited since I don't like it at all.
I awoke about a day later when the room phone rang
In a motel where Elvis had stayed, the Roadway Inn.
I've had less than one beer ever, the last with a Muslim;
A few mixed drinks; I don't even like them.
I don't even care for wine at communion;
Yet in court it was said I'd been drinking.

Hating alcohol likely saved my life;
Hating it saves many from trouble and strife.
As for pills or drugs, I took about as many two times
As I have taken during all my life combined.
Betrayed and judged while being me,
But I later got a PsyD and MD.

*See poem "Daddy Drunk with Guns"

Valentine-ation

Excitement and exhilaration
Flirtation and infatuation
Obsession and fascination
Magical prestidigitation
Passion and consummation
Ejaculation and exclamation
Orgasmic ultimate sensation
Education and experimentation
Hearing bells, tintinnabulation
Wishing for a celebration
Beautification and desecration
Beatification and demonization
Carefree and careless contamination
Dissipation and degeneration
Alienation and damnation
Disappointment and desolation
Emancipation and exploitation
Relocation and reunification
Calumniation and confabulation
Scarring cicatrization
Errors and Eros, Electra-fication
Insanity, irrationalization
Generations a perpetuation
Of past and future civilization.

Honey

Honey from the buzzing bee
Sweetest nectar known to me.
Taste the honey on one's lips;
Feel desire between one's hips.
Let's forget the stinging bee;
Remember rawest, purest ecstasy
Honey, sweetness, come to me;
Forget about the killer bee.

Flies and Butterflies

What's all this about the fly
And its buzz heard when you die?
Seems silly, but I know it's true;
A fly shows up out of the blue;
At times like when a mean man dies;
And, strangely, there appears a fly;
Like in my kitchen the biggest fly;
After the funeral when a brother died;
And in the room upon the death
When a killer took his last breath.

And, whoa! Look there! Two big flies!
Buzzing around where an old aunt lies.
Is it John and Junior, her son and his,
Buzzing around, not missing this?
Or is one she, a fly, no less,
Paying her debt for stealing the dress?

Then there are butterflies some see;
If not a fly or ant or bee;
Appearing on the funeral day
Of a loved one in the month of May;
Or any other time of year.
So we wonder if what we hear
Means there's truth to what some say?

Can You Mark a Baby?

I never really considered this until the other day.
Heard a woman who wrote a book about a factory.
What could this possibly have to do with a baby?
(Reminds me that some called grandma a baby factory.)

Seems a factory worker got burned on her arm
When she was with child, and it left three scars;
Then when her baby boy was born,
On his arm were three similar birthmarks.

The curious book writer, who was quite perplexed,
Asked "Can you mark a baby?" to a Harvard biologist.
The biologist boldly answered, somewhat vexed,
"Of course not; no way; it's not possible."

Then I recalled how my mother used to say
Old people like her mama thought you could mark a baby
By things you said and did when you were expecting,
Especially bad things you might be resurrecting.

Mother laughed and told about the hamburgers she'd crave,
And the birthmark on my forehead I will take to my grave.
If Harvard says so I guess you can't be hexed,
But as for me (and maybe the writer), I'm still perplexed.

Twenty Humans Who Saved Millions*

Edward Jenner, an English physician scientist who died in 1823,
Is considered the father of immunology.
He's credited with developing the smallpox vaccine;
Although it had been widely used before then;
Well before Jenner it was used by Benjamin Franklin.
Jenner tested it the most and wrote scientific papers;
Told how he scraped pus from cowpox on milkmaid fingers;
Injected many subjects and they were survivors.
Napoleon thus had his troops vaccinated and released English prisoners.

Joseph Lister of England and Louis Pasteur in France
Were most notable in their time medical scientists.
Oliver Wendell Holmes in the US, Ignaz Semmelweiss in Hungary
Were notable, too, as was Robert Koch in Germany;
All medical scientists in the mid-to-late 19th century.
Lister is sometimes cited as being the first surgeon
To suggest disease is transferred by what doctors are touching.
It seems a no-brainer now; it was controversial back then.
Lister called the father of antiseptic technique and surgery that's modern.
Lister learned from reading a paper by Louis Pasteur.
Pasteur was a chemist, not a physician like the other four;
Pasteur called "the father of microbiology";
He, too, had his doubters and controversy.
He developed his famous germ theory;
His work helped prevent much disease,
And he developed the anthrax and rabies vaccines.
Holmes in Boston, before Lister or Pasteur,
Warned about spreading childbirth fever.
He said to burn exposed clothing and purify instruments.
His warnings went a little too far for some physicians,
When he said, if exposed, "Don't deliver babies for six months."
Semmelweiss warned a little later to "wash your hands"
After handling a cadaver before touching live humans.

13

He, too, was concerned about childbirth fever,
More common in hospital births after handling a cadaver.
He became mentally ill and rather obsessed;
And died at age 47 of pyemia after being beaten and stressed.
Koch came along after the other four were grown;
A microbiologist, for four postulates known.
He's considered the father of modern bacteriology;
And identified the causes of anthrax, cholera, and TB.
Holmes and Semmelweiss might have directly saved fewer,
But I thought they deserved credit with Koch, Lister, and Pasteur.

Fritz Haber, a Jewish German in 1918,
Got the Nobel Prize in Chemistry for ammonia making.
It's used in explosives and fertilizer, too,
Helping grow much of the world's food.

Henrietta Lacks of Virginia, who died at age 31 in 1951,
Was unaware of how famous she would become.
Her rare cervical cancer cells were deadly to her,
But the first immortalized cells found saved many others.
Her "HeLa" cells used in space and the world's laboratories;
Helping millions survive due to medical breakthroughs;
Helping many not suffer and die from polio;
Helping many to live due to fertilization in-vitro.

Alan Turing, an English genius cryptanalyst, died in 1954;
A biologist, logician, mathematician, philosopher, and more.
Called the father of theoretical computer science
And the founder of artificial intelligence.
A Cambridge man and PhD from Princeton in 1938;
Cracked the Enigma code before it was even more too late;
Else Germany could have won the war or fought two years more.
Some say he saved 14 million lives and saved the world.
Sadly, Turing couldn't save himself from cyanide;
After chemical castration he was an apparent suicide.

Jonas Salk, an American, invented the polio vaccine in 1955,
Which means millions more people are now alive.
He worked on a polio project started by President FDR;

He was known as a genius, expected to go far.
Salk was a man of great principle, of moral commitment;
Though he could have made billions, he wouldn't get a patent.
He worked in several laboratories in those scary days.
He established in California The Salk Institute.
Hardly anyone is considered more admired or astute.
At the end of his life worked on a vaccine for HIV/AIDS.

Vasili Arkhipov, a Soviet officer near Cuba in 1962,
Must have been a man who kept his cool.
Aboard a nuclear-armed submarine detecting depth charges;
The American Navy was trying to get the sub to surface.
For all the Soviets knew they were under attack,
For they were too deep for radio contact.
The other two officers on board and the captain, too,
Agreed to launch a nuclear torpedo.
It took only one to be rightly decisive;
Arkhipov might have saved the world in the Cuban Missile Crisis.

Stanislav Petrov in the USSR in 1983
Was a nuclear early-warning center's officer on duty.
Rather than a premature retaliation,
He rightly ruled an alarm was wrong;
Preventing nuclear war and Armageddon;
Petrov saved millions in his and our nation.

Alexei Ananenko, Boris Baranov, and Valeri Bezpalov, in 1986 in Ukraine,
Were three men at Chernobyl who would save millions again.
Ten days after the nuclear power plant meltdown,
There was great danger there of another explosion.
It could send across most of Europe radioactive steam
Unless some stepped up to face great harm.
Ananenko, Baranov, and Bezpalov
Volunteered to open the safety valves,
Knowing it would mean sure death for themselves.
They saved many others but suffered and died two weeks later;
A big reason to have doubts about using nuclear power.

Boris Yeltsin, Russian president in 1995,

15

Deserves great credit for keeping many alive.
After Norwegian and American scientists launched
a research rocket from Norway,
On a threatening trajectory in a corridor that included Moscow.
Yeltsin opened his nuclear suitcase, but didn't
give the Russian order for "Go!"
First time a nuclear state has ever gone so far as far as we know.

Maurice Hilleman, an American microbiologist who died in 2005,
Of all scientists in the 20th century might have saved more lives.
Helped find viruses that cause cancer, the common cold, and hepatitis;
He developed vaccines for chickenpox, measles, mumps, meningitis,
Hepatitis A and hepatitis B, a type of pneumonia, and HIB.
Hilleman's been called the greatest vaccinologist in history.

Norman Borlaug, an American biologist who died in 2009,
Is also known as a Nobel laureate and humanitarian.
He's been called "the father of the Green Revolution"
And "agriculture's greatest spokesperson,"
Who might have saved a billion people from starvation.
He managed to combine better production and high-yield wheat,
So many in need around the world could have food to eat.

James Harrison of Australia is still alive,
Along with over two million others he helped survive.
His blood plasma contains a rare enzyme
That has saved many babies time after time;
Babies and mothers with a Rhesus factor problem;
Mothers needing anti-D globulin, known as Rhogam,
So her immune system won't fight the fetus.
Harrison has donated about 1,000 times over fifty years;
He vowed after heart surgery as a teen he'd be a donor,
And his rare enzyme even saved his own daughter.

Kary Mullis from nearby Lenoir, North Carolina,
In 1993 shared the Nobel Prize in Chemistry;
Mullis for inventing the polymerase chain reaction,
Which can amplify DNA in hours rather than days by millions;
Which greatly accelerated the Human Genome Project.

He might have gotten an idea while on LSD;
He's known for being a little wild and crazy.
All the benefits are hard to imagine,
Like treating cancers with molecular medicine;
And treating viruses through genotyping;
Reducing risk and bioprocessing;
Biofuels and other forms of energy;
Implications for agriculture and animal husbandry.
(Don't begin to think, though, that I'd suggest LSD)
All the benefits haven't come to fruition,
But it seems likely they'll save more than a million.

*Sources are **https://kindnessblogdotcom1.iles.wordpress.com/2014/03/
uniform_expanded.jpg**; and Wikipedia; obtained September 7, 2017.

Elvis and Nixon

Graceland in Memphis was missing Elvis
Just a few days before Christmas,
When he took off in 1970
To see the president in Washington DC.

Elvis took with him a guard or two,
And in the airport they got through
With a Colt-45 Christmas gift for Nixon,
A special Elvis hand-picked handgun.

In the airport Elvis met a soldier
Coming home from the Vietnam War.
Of course, Elvis gave him all his cash--
Five hundred dollars; Elvis was generous.

Elvis had once been a soldier, too.
At the peak of his fame he, too, was drafted;
And some people said his career was through.
Had he not been so great would he have lasted?

On the plane Elvis wrote Nixon a note.
On the War on Drugs Nixon had Elvis' vote.
This was and was not quite ironic,
For Elvis was a prescription drug addict.

Downers to sleep, uppers to awake,
A big mistake that many make;
A vicious cycle, a not-fun game;
Sometimes a pattern of the victims of fame.

It seems that Elvis was on a mission.
Is dissatisfaction a human condition?
Is that why many seek religion?
Elvis, like many, felt something was missing.

18

Elvis collected law officer badges for whatever reason;
Maybe because his father had been in prison.
Sometimes Elvis would stop people for speeding;
A sight to see, whether serious or kidding.

In DC in the White House Nixon had no idea
That Elvis Presley was anywhere near;
But in a few hours it was arranged
For Elvis Presley to meet Richard Nixon.

Elvis sat down in Nixon's of all the chairs.
Sat at Nixon's desk; helped himself to souvenirs.
Elvis said it was funny how George Washington dressed.
Nixon said, "Elvis, you're dressed a little unusual yourself."

Nixon the President but Elvis the King;
Elvis wearing more than one big ring;
Elvis in a royal purple suit made of velvet,
With a cape, no less, and a big-buckled belt.

Got in the Oval Office and gave the gun gift.
Gave Nixon his note, against drug crime committed;
And got the federal agent's badge that he wanted.
Those superstars, they sure are quite different.

About the King

Let me tell you about the King
And what happened when he'd sing.
The most exciting thing we'd ever see;
Made us happy; felt so free.

I knew he had it before I knew what it was;
Seeing this feast for my heart, ears, and eyes.
He sang and shook and rocked and rolled;
Shook us up and stirred our souls.

We put his pictures on our walls;
He picked us up through all our falls.
Men would come and men would go,
But he was there wherever we'd go.

When he left we grieved and cried;
Then we knew he hadn't died.
He lived inside us through it all;
Long live the King of rock and roll.

Ballads, blues, love songs, gospel, soul;
Heartbreak Hotel, Paralyzed, How Great Thou Art,
Don't Be Cruel, Love Me, Don't, In the Ghetto...;
To me he'll always be a part.

Wow!

—◦◦⊙✕⊙◦◦—

I know this seems silly,
But it's also eerie
And more than a little strange;
But I'm writing about possible aliens.

We've all heard of Roswell
And that the government won't tell;
So, we read stories of Area 51,
And if there really were aliens.
A story I found a little plausible
Is that a hovercraft came from Russia;
With three teenagers as I recall;
Landed at Roswell to cause shock and awe;
Surgically changed to not look like humans,
So people would think they were really aliens;
A witness saw them dying and dead;
Saw Russian letters, at least one story said.

Nearly forty years ago at Ohio State
The Big Ear Radio Telescope, somehow,
Caught a seventy-two second signal called "Wow!"
The only such signal detected to-date.
The mystery remains still today
From far away in the Milky Way;
A possible signal from extraterrestrials
Or for the religious, from far-away celestials.
The date was August 15, 1977,
The day before Elvis went to Heaven.
Or was he picked up by a spacecraft alien?
Or are his remains only at Graceland?

Melvin McKinney Is His Name

He could have had fortune;
He could have had fame;
I want you to know him;
Melvin McKinney is his name.

Born the same year as Elvis, in '35;
Making music in the '50s; what a time to be alive!
I remember the day he came to our school
To put on a show; he was so cool.

Parked his nearly new Cadillac under a tree
Where no one dared park; must be a VIP!
Some said he sang Cash songs better than Cash;
I was star struck and got his autograph.

I thought he'd be really famous one day,
For to me he had all that it takes;
And like Elvis, it seemed he was well on his way;
But then, somehow, he didn't get the breaks.

He played for free at a local beer joint
Just so he could play his guitar and sing.
The size of the stage wasn't the point,
But I guess had had thoughts of what could have been.

I'm sure he looked back, with talent to spare;
His life unfulfilled, ending with despair.
He got real sick and drove an old fishing car;
Then he stopped singing and put away his guitar.

He died at age 40, with too much to bear.
I hope he's in Heaven singing somewhere
With Elvis and Johnny Cash and June Carter,
And others like them, in a Heavenly choir.

He should have had fortune;
He should have had fame;
I want you to know him;
Melvin McKinney is his name.

America by Greyhound

(can sing to the tune of "America the Beautiful")

America, America, I saw from the seat of a Greyhound bus.
No telling what you'll see or hear.
I hope you feel peace and don't feel fear.

I rode Greyhound from El Paso;
You wouldn't believe what I did in Mexico.
Our young twin boys were way back East;
I could hardly wait to give them their treat.

They're like Elvis and Jesse, had Jesse lived;
I was really hoping they'd like their gift;
Hoping someday they'll sing in a show
And play their guitars I bought in Mexico.

People looked at the guitars sticking out of my bags;
I clutched them tight, fearing thieves in the night.
There were people well-dressed and people in rags;
Guess some hated flying or couldn't afford a flight.

Some people looked kind, others happy, sad, or tough;
As we stopped at every dusty Texas town, it seemed.
At an early stop they took some Mexicans off;
Would they get another chance at the American dream?

America, America, I saw from the seat of a Greyhound bus.
No telling what you'll see or hear.
You may feel sad; you may shed a tear.

Through Dallas/Ft Worth I thought of a lover
And how he decided to be with another.
"I'm just a bad Texan," he gave as a reason,
As he guzzled a beer and prepared for deer season.

The scariest sight was a bloody Texan;
Nope, it wasn't a "bad hombre" Mexican;
Said it was hog blood on his pants we'd see;
Wonder why at the next stop picked up by police?

I sat by the widow of a World War II soldier.
She told how they lived back during the war;
And built on their lives with faith in the future;
Her stories were food for my soul half-starved.

Then we saw a sign saying Hope, Arkansas;
Couldn't help but think how far one can go
In this country of ours, thanks to true heroes
Who sweat when they work, save lives, fight our wars.
(And I thought of Bill Clinton I liked, also.)

A cursing, angry case, perhaps on PCP,
Seemed a shame to himself, our country, mankind;
Was also forced off, likely lucky for me,
For I was about to ask him about his mind.
(Or was he about to get a piece of my mind?)

America, America, I saw from the seat of a Greyhound bus.
No telling what you'll see or hear.
You may feel tired; you may feel fear.

A serious student was reading a book;
She studied and studied and hardly looked up;
She was in her fifties and in medical school;
Still seeking her dream, where goodness can rule.

A missionary going to Zimbabwe
Seemed surprised to see a pyramid in Tennessee.
"You see, it's in America's Memphis," I said;
"The home of my King, Elvis Presley."

Two women were kissing, not seeing our eyes.
A schizophrenic swatted unseen flies.
A cowboy who had played with Hank Junior and Waylon

25

Was going to Nashville to try to make a living.

After thirty-six hours with no sleep but with dreams,
It was good to see Asheville and my family;
Good to hug our boys who started plucking the strings
In this crazy, great country with so much to see and be.

**America, America, I saw from the seat of a Greyhound bus.
No telling what you'll see or hear.
I hope you have peace and hold it dear.**

Glen Campbell Died Today

Glen Campbell died today and to my surprise;
He was the third singer whose death made me cry.
I was nearly five when Hank Williams died and I cried;
And forty years ago this month was when Elvis died.
Sure, I've been sad when others have gone;
Their music has helped us feel less alone.
Some may say many others as great,
But I don't see music as a matter to debate.
Glen Campbell brought us the Good Time Hour;
And for that hour every Sunday night,
We could forget about the news of the Vietnam fight.
Glen and others helped us through those troubling days;
Among them Pete Seeger and Bob Dylan and Joan Baez.
I think Glen said because he was the seventh son of a seventh son
That he was lucky; I know our hearts he won;
Singing songs like "Rhinestone Cowboy" and "Galveston."
A Beach Boy awhile; man, could he talk and sing and play;
Played for many, even Sinatra and Elvis back in the day;
And Glen, like those greats, did it his way.
When Glen started to forget he could remember to play and sing;
Maybe that's one reason I find it so touching.

Now I'm starting to reminisce
About all the others that we miss.
I can't even begin to name all the greats;
Like John Lennon and George Harrison, half of the Beatles;
But we still have Ringo Starr and Paul McCartney.
Hank Sr long gone but we still have Hank Jr.
There are only two left of The Highwaymen;
We've lost Johnny Cash and Waylon Jennings,
But we still have Willie Nelson and Kris Kristofferson.
We lost Chuck Berry but still have Jerry Lee Lewis.
Some we still have are now mostly our memories.

We've lost Glenn Frey but we still have Vince Gill.
We've lost "Golden Ring's" Tammy Wynette and George Jones;
With little harmony at home but harmony in songs.
We have still in love Tim McGraw and Faith Hill.
We've lost Merle Haggard, Okie from Muskogee and Bakersfield.
We lost Whitney Houston but still have Tom Jones;
No better singers of many love songs.
We still have Kenny Rogers and Dolly Parton.
"I Will Always Love You," making Dolly a downright icon.
(Be sure to see Mylie as "Dolly" doing
"Islands in the Stream" with "Kenny" Jimmy Fallon.)
Not all we still have are still recording;
But now great Garth Brooks has again started touring.
And I saw Charlie Pride again recently singing;
Saw him in concert when we still had segregation;
When he couldn't stay in some hotels or eat in some restaurants;
Or blacks like him attend many schools in our nation.

I also think of the beloved Johnny Cash Show;
In front of the TV our whole family would go;
With June Carter Cash and her family, the Carters,
Country music founding mothers and fathers.
I've seen some of them in person, King Elvis, of course;
But the one I've seen the most was Johnny Cash.
Once in concert at the height of his fame;
Once at a Billy Graham Crusade at the Georgia Dome;
Once in Atlanta at the Fox Theater with the Highwaymen.
Once saw him walking out of a New York City hotel;
We might have seen famous others, but how could we tell?
If they weren't on TV we wouldn't know;
None of us had ever been to a Broadway show.

I saw Tom Jones three times in person when he was on TV;
All three times were a thrill for me.
The first time in the new town of Columbia, Maryland;
His opening act was Gladys Knight and the Pips;
In the audience was a drunken, jealous husband
Who started mocking Tom Jones and wiggling his hips.
The last time his opening act was George Wallace, the comedian;

Funnier for it was in Montgomery where the governor had the same name.
I saw Kenny Rogers twice; once in concert, another time in Georgia.
He passed me driving a maroon Cadillac,
drinking from a long-necked bottle.
I'm not sure but I might have seen Hank Jr twice;
Once when he finished his concert he mooned us;
Possibly again when a man asked me if I wanted a ride;
When the maroon Mercedes pulled away the tag said "Bocephus."
(Yes, both of those cars I mentioned were maroon.
My favorite car color, too, not just music in common.)

I didn't see Ray Charles or Stevie Wonder (nor them me),
But I've had "Georgia on my mind" and think of "Ebony and Ivory."
I haven't seen Lionel Ritchie but I'm glad he's still singing and wrote "Lady."
(I've been in his home with his piano where he
lived with his grandma in Tuskegee.)
We no longer see the Oak Ridge Boys or hear "Elvira";
Or the Gatlin Brothers sing about "All the Gold in California."
There was oft played Ben E King and Percy Sledge for a time;
And James Taylor's song of Carolina and Neil Diamond's "Sweet Caroline";
Bob Seger and the Silver Bullet Band when we
were "Running Against the Wind";
Elton John when we feel like a "Candle in the Wind";
And Simon and Garfunkel when we're crossing
a "Bridge Over Troubled Water";
Or the Statler Brothers Quartet when we were
"Counting Flowers on the Wall"
And wished our names were Mary Lou; or
Lisa when we heard Jesse Coulter;
But not Norma Jean or Princess Diana when we
heard Sir Elton John again in awe;
Thought of "Whispering Pines" and "All for the
Love of a Girl" by Johnny Horton
When going "North to Alaska" when my grand-daughter was born.
So many great singers and songs, I can't name them all.
Once I heard that the top country song was Tammy's "Stand By Your Man";
Women also need to listen to Helen Reddy's strong anthem "I Am Woman";
Bruce Springsteen makes us glad we were "Born in the USA";
I adore him and his music; what more can I say?

The Dixie Chicks were so good and strong
when the Iraqi War was so wrong.
Alan Jackson helped us through with "Where Were You?" after 9/11.
I like the songs on the tape I bought in New Orleans called "Super Cajun";
And Bryan Adams singing about really loving a woman.
Have hardly wasted away in Jimmy Buffet's Margaritaville;
But I stepped in the rain, not in flip flops, to try to sell a song in Nashville.
There's talented Taylor Swift, and Adele giving her great voice a rest;
Can't remember when I've heard greats Reba
and Jewel and Alanis Morissette.
Hear Carrie Underwood, Chris Stapleton,
Keith Urban, Florida Georgia Line;
Dierks Bentley, Brad Paisley, Miranda Lambert,
Blake Shelton and Luke Bryan.
We still love Shania Twain's "Man, I Feel Like a Woman";
And when we hear Cat Stevens sing "Morning Has Broken";
John Denver is gone but fills our senses with "Annie's Song."
Like Lady Antebellum's "Need You Now," "Girl
Crush" took it all for Little Big Town.

When I lived in St Lucia there was rasta and raggae,
Like the belief and music of Bob Marley in Jamaica;
With "Jah is my co-pilot" on the tags of some cars;
But it was country music you'd hear coming from bars.
I was utterly surprised to hear a country music station
Play old but popular country music on that island nation.
Legendary Bob Marley and the Wailers I must praise;
Their songs still with much meaning in these troubled days.
"Get Up, Stand Up"; "Stir It Up";
"Lively Up Yourself"'; "Cheer Up";
"One Love" reminds us we all need loving;
Don't shoot the sheriff or the deputy; don't shoot anyone.
Reminds me of a great Youngblood song from 1967;
We need to "Get Together" to make Earth more like Heaven.

In reminiscing I've left out a host
But these are some I heard the most.
I've just gone back and wanted to tell
About some of them, like Glen Campbell.

George Jones sang, "Who's Gonna Fill Their Shoes?"
We still have recordings; they we won't lose.
We lost Michael Jackson and Prince and other stars,
But we still have others like Beyonce and Bruno Mars.
We've seen Justin Bieber growing up and singing he's "Sorry."
Not long ago awesome Alicia Keys sang with young Maren Morris;
And darling Dolly Parton sang "Jolene" with god-daughter Mylie Cyrus.
Yes, I love Mylie Cyrus and now Noah and, as always, Billy Ray.
(I happen to love his new "Thin Line" CD, his
"Some Gave All" and "Achy Breaky.")
We'll never forget Martina McBride and "Independence Day."
Freddie Mercury died but Adam Lambert great with Queen.
Others rise up and life goes on, and other great ones come along.

Serving Time

Serving time in federal prison,
A pretty girl got ten long years.
She rode that long, black train to nowhere;
She didn't think of her parents' fears.
Her parents feared she'd lose her children,
Her life, her home, her dreams they feared.
Her parents tried to keep her out of prison;
They wouldn't tell how she took from them.
She's far from home in a women's prison;
From her Southern roots to a Northern jail.
Her children cry to see their mommy,
But they are way too young to tell.
Was Daddy, too, doing wrong with Mommy?
And did he really cheat and such?
They lost their home and one another;
Their jobs, their car, they lost so much.
They crashed and burned and hit rock bottom.
He raked and scraped and crawled from Hell.
She dealt and stole and dug in deeper;
She didn't think she would go to jail.
Their parents helped their troubled children,
And they helped raise the little ones.
So if you're thinking drugs are cool,
You're such a fool. This is so true.
Serving time in federal prison,
A Southern girl got ten long years.
She rode that long, black train to nowhere;
And she now thinks of her parents' fears.

Martha and Marty*

Alderson, Alderson,
Not a place to have much fun.
Martha's there, it seems unfair;
The men go free, the feds don't care.

Marty's there from way down South.
She sold drugs, she ran her mouth.
A dang fool girl, messed up her life;
Wants to be back home and be a wife.

Martha and Marty share a room
With little in common but a mop and broom.
They try to talk to lift the gloom;
Two poor souls in a prison room.

"Hey, welcome to prison, ma'am, what's your crime?
You'll be the latest bunk mate of mine."
"My name's Martha, and I sold drug stock."
"What is drug stock? Mama went to Woodstock."

"My name's Marty, and I sold drugs, too."
[Martha] "But I didn't sell drugs like you
I sold on the stock market, not on the streets.
Look at the holes in these sheets."

[Marty] "I wrote bad checks." [Martha] "I sent e-mail."
[Both] "I didn't think I'd go to jail."
[Marty] "I was banned from the market." [Martha] "And I was, too.
I'm rich and famous you little fool."

[Marty] "I like to shop and I really miss Walmart."
[Martha] "I miss New York; I sell to K Mart.
Don't you know who I am?"
[Marty] "When you're in prison we don't give a ham."

[Marty] "We get three meals a day in a big lunch room."
[Martha] "What time is dinner?" [Marty] "It's at 12 o'clock noon."
[Martha] "I call that lunch." [Marty] "And then there's supper.
[Martha] "Guess there's no brunch." [Marty] "I could use an upper."
[Marty] "It's called Camp Cupcake." [Martha] "It's more like corn cake.
I need some rum cake. I hope they'll let me cook and bake."

"I'm from down South from a place called New Fort,
With two red lights and no airport."
"I'm from up North and have a place in Newport;
I wish I could stay in the nearby resort."

[Martha] "These beds are bad; the rooms are small."
[Marty] "We share the big bathroom down the hall.
I miss watching TV." [Martha] "I miss doing TV."
[Both] "I want to go home; I want to be free."

They cook and clean and sweep and mop;
Sometimes they think they're gonna drop.
Supper at six, lights out at eight;
At least there's not a fence and gate.

Marty mixed colors doing laundry one day;
Martha's white socks now pink for an obvious reason
"Didn't your mother tell you how to sort laundry?"
(If she'd listened to her mama she wouldn't be in prison.)

[Marty] "I hate housework, don't you too?"
[Martha] "I'm famous for housework, you little fool.
You really don't know who I am?"
.[Marty] "You're a pris'ner here, like I am, ma'am."

[Marty] "Sometimes we get to go out in the yard,
And make phone calls if we can buy a card.
They cost more here than they do back home;
Guess these people want to make them some."

[Marty] "What's your house like? Mine was a double wide.
It used to have wheels but you couldn't take a ride."

[Martha] "I have four homes and lots of pride,
And what in the world is a double wide?"

Alderson, Alderson, not a place to have much fun.
But did Martha say Marty helped make her grin?
Martha's white socks may no longer be wearable,
But did Martha say Marty helped make prison bearable?

*The conversations herein are only from the poet's imagination.

Sticks and Stones

Sticks and stones can break your bones,
but words can break your heart;
Watch your words; don't let them hurt; don't tear a soul apart.

When each one came into the world its soul was pure and strong.
In a few short years how is it that some things can go so wrong?
If we're made to feel we're bad and that we're not worth love,
We may become like those who would even kill a dove.
(Then sometimes all the love and care in the world
May not be enough to fix a troubled boy or girl.)

Sticks and stones can break your bones,
but words can break your heart;
Watch your words; don't let them hurt; don't tear a soul apart.

Someone who's dif'rent may feel shame for no good reason at all;
Because someone said a mean name;
"So what if I'm skinny, fat, short, or tall?
What if I'm sick in my body or head, and what if I don't want to fight?
Don't make me wish that I was dead.
Don't put me down; you have no right!
What if I talk "funny" or with an accent or I stutter?
It's my heart and soul and feelings that should matter.
What if I'm not great at singing or dancing or sports or I'm clumsy?
Let me have fun and enjoy life, too; don't make fun of me.
What if I don't seem bright or what if I seem too bright?"
We used to say, "Mind your beeswax" and "Go fly a kite."
"What if I'm a boy and want to be a girl,
or a man who loves a man, or vice versa?
Don't think I need your preaching on how I shouldn't be my own person."

Sticks and stones can break your bones,
but words can break your heart;
Watch your words; don't let them hurt; don't tear a soul apart.

One may be rich and one may be poor,
But money's not a measure of one's character.
If someone says you're ugly, what do they know?
What is ugly is their words; they're no a mirror to your soul.
If someone puts you down and you want to just give up;
He may be putting you down just to raise his low self up.
Two lovers who are breaking up may just cause more pain.
They only end up hurting more; there's nothing that they gain.

Sticks and stones can break your bones,
but words can break your heart;
Watch your words; don't let them hurt; don't tear a soul apart.
Don't let words scar you and tear you apart;
Be true to yourself and be kind in your heart.

The Revival

—◦❊◦—

He had a loving mama, but they didn't go to church;
Since he didn't have a daddy they were shamed; they didn't have much.
He was six or seven when the big tent came to town;
He thought it was the circus and he'd get to see a clown.
When he heard it was a preacher he still wished to go;
His mama called it a revival, said it's not a circus show.
They put on their best clothes, and they walked into town;
He didn't understand why some people stared and frowned.
Since his Mama held her head down he just went along,
And they sat on the back row just like they did not belong.
They could hardly wait to hear the well-known preacher speak;
When he spoke they both looked up; the boy was barely on the seat.
The preacher said to always love the Lord and one another;
The boy liked what he heard and scooted closer to his mother.
When the preacher stopped his preaching he walked down the aisle;
He looked right at the boy, and he asked, to their surprise;
"Boy, where's your Daddy?" I don't know why;
He said, "I don't have a daddy," and he looked like he would cry.
The boy put his head down, and his Mama did, too;
Then the preacher said real loud, "You know your father loves you.
You have a good mama and a Heavenly Father, boy";
Then the boy raised his head, and he cried and cried with joy.
The revival that night helped form a boy's fate,
And he became the governor of a United State.
So, hold your head up, every girl and boy;
Try to love one another, and to only cry with joy.
Hold your head up, every girl and boy;
Try to love one another, and to only cry with joy.

38

Killing Ourselves

Care for your body; care for the Earth,
Or the next generation is doomed at birth.
We keep killing ourselves with so much excess;
Polluting the air with coal, oil and gas.

Food and drink and drugs and smoke;
We laugh and play like it's just a joke.
Waste, waste, waste, there the atmosphere goes;
While we buy, buy, buy too many clothes.
We think we need a big SUV
To carry home our latest big-screen TV
To our big overheated, over-cooled home;
Forgetting that Earth is facing doom.
China may finish off the Earth,
Burning their coal to make our stuff;
Stuff we don't need but it's frequently sold
At the nearby Walmart just down the road.

We pay, pay, pay for the addicts and users,
The criminals, cheaters, liars, abusers,
The entitled, the exploiters, the wasteful, the rulers;
Their wars, their wrongs, but ridiculing improvers.
We have unsafe sex, get abortions and AIDS;
We even waste fetuses; these are insane days.
We're heating the Earth, causing drought and storm;
Fifty million refugees are now the norm.
All the waste is a big disgrace;
Even the old who don't know their child's face.
We spend trillions on senseless wars;
Killing many, even civilians, and our own soldiers.
The poor they resent us, but it gives them no right
To behead and bomb and take a life.
We're extremists, too, causing senseless death
Of our bodies and Earth with all our excess.

Clean up your act; clean up your life;
Clean up the earth; clean up your mind;
Care for your body; care for the Earth;
Care for the children; care for mankind.

Before the Pill

—◦◦⟨◉⟩◦◦—

In the days before the Pill
More babies born against one's will;
Many families ten or more;
Many hungry, tired and poor.

Birth control illegal 'til '65;
Not 1775 but 1965;
Independence in 1776;
Not really until 1966.

One Grandma born in 1888,
Wed at 13; today it's rape;
With child at that, the father 20;
A child herself; it happened to plenty.

Fourteen babies born to them;
Never knew how to practice rhythm.
Even though a new invention;
But illegal to use the condom.

Roe versus Wade in 1973
Another way to be set free;
Fewer coat hangers, still the grief;
Remember responsibility.

Guilt About Grandma

She was born March 4, 1879;
Ten days before Albert Einstein.
She died at age eighty-seven
Several years after she lost her mind;
She got senile dementia, whatever the cause;
Don't know if she even remembered Santa Claus.
For awhile stayed a month at each child's home;
Sometimes she got my little brother's room;
Sometimes she slept in my room with me;
I was a silly teen and way too modest;
And didn't want Grandma to see me undress;
I wouldn't even let her see me in my slip;
But hated how she said, "I'll leave and let you strip."
One winter when a brother was home from the Army,
Someone got the great idea (not male chivalry)
That Grandma could get the cot, and Mother could sleep with me
In the very cold back bedroom that had no heat.
And at her own son's funeral she got a second-row seat;
Sat behind his wife and children and the family's maid.
My mother thought that was a disgrace;
Maybe because the maid was black; maybe not about race.
Grandma could still sing and remember do re mi;
The music and its methods she learned as a girl.
Just think of all the changes Grandma would see
Through all the years that she lived in this world.
Grandma started to imagine things that weren't true;
Like she had visited her son and grandsons in Europe in World War II;
And while she was on her trip traveling there,
She thought she also met General Eisenhower.

What a full life she had, though nothing like Einstein's;
She raised a big family in the North Carolina mountains.
She birthed nine children; only one died as a child;
He was about two, soon after the nearby 1916 flood;

42

Two strong-willed girls, seven handful sons;
She kept a cow she milked and also raised chickens;
She gathered Galax she sold, and eggs and butter;
And she'd wring a chicken's neck for Sunday dinner.
Like most local families, she had no maid;
She'd take the children to help work in the field.
And when her own children got grown,
She'd go to others' homes and help deliver their children.
Grandpa worked at the quarry and had a farm;
Grandma and Grandpa were a hard-working team.
She supported his decision when they didn't have much
To give $500 to building the Methodist church.
I doubt he made a hundred dollars a month,
And I'm sure it was much more than a tenth.
It's where we had our reunion, maybe my last;
Where Grandma taught the women's Sunday school class.

Grandma would defend those handful boys;
"Among 'em said" Grandma was part of the problem;
She would feign a heart attack and make wailful noise
When Grandpa got his belt to discipline them.
(So much for Grandma and Grandpa Swofford making a team.)

Grandpa's father died when he was fifteen;
And Grandma's mother had four children by four men.
When they met she was barefoot, he liked to tell;
He left out that she already had a little child.
They rose from little to have a lot of land;
All the way from the highway to the top of the mountain;
And they went on to have many grand-children;
Maybe we should have another reunion.

A favorite story was about during the Great Depression,
And perhaps one of my greatest life lessons.
Grandma would see strangers walking down the road,
And invite them to her house to have some food.
This wasn't any food--it was food they raised;
Working hard to have it; still to God they praised.
No bathroom or running water in the kitchen;

And certainly no maid or slave or servant.
They got water from a pail lifted from a nearby well;
Went to the bathroom in an outdoor toilet or another pail;
Can you imagine if we had to do that now?
Raised and killed the pig and chickens and cow,
And whatever wildlife that happened to be near;
Squirrels, possums, coons, turkeys, bear, deer.
As far as I know, Grandma never shot a gun,
But several of her boys loved dogs and guns and to hunt.
She kept cured hams and such in the smokehouse,
But not a killed snake or any kind of mouse.
They raised their own vegetables and fruits,
And it would take all day to crack a jar of walnuts.
And when it was hottest in the summer it was time to can
With wood you cut yourself for the stove in the kitchen.
Of course, for many years there was no gas stove or electricity,
Which meant Grandma did so much with no modern conveniences.
Grandma made sorghum molasses she kept in a barrel in a closet;
One time she found in the bottom of the barrel the missing cat.

When Grandma lived with us when I was a teen
I'm so ashamed of being so mean;
And tho' I went to her Methodist church every Sunday,
I don't know why we didn't take Grandma that day.
She asked me after church if there was a good crowd;
I'm sure she would have loved to have heard about it, but I said,
"I guess it was a crowd, but I don't know if they are good."
Don't know why because Grandma was a relic
I thought it gave me the right to be a smart aleck.
I don't know why we couldn't take any grandmother;
We were supposedly Christian and should know to be better.
The elderly often deserve more respect,
And none of them deserve abuse and neglect.
I wish instead of that cold cot I had stood up for her;
Said the warmest, best bed should be for our grandmother;
And I wish I had sat down with her and listened more
About her home remedies or whatever story.
You may get old and forgetful, too;
Remember to follow the Golden Rule.

44

I feel much guilt about her now.
I can still remember her calling her cow;
And we still remember how she smelled of butter;
And her peaches in the winter from her summer canning;
Older siblings and cousins remember her great cooking;
And her saying "Don't say anything bad about another";
And we remember how she sang when she was dying.

She'd tell my sisters, "Love your husbands; I sure miss Pa";
She cared for him for years when he was in a wheelchair,
After he had a stroke, when she said they were making love;
I think if anyone's there, they're together in Heaven above.

Julia Ann Josephine Amelia Green

Julia Ann Josephine Amelia Green,
What was it that you dared to dream?
Born in 1888,
Wed at 13; today it's rape.
With child at that, named Vera May,
Born in May and dead in June;
Then Spencer, Walter, Nellie Jane,
Louise and Lawrence, James and Blanche;
Did any of them have a chance?
Two years between and three more died;
I guess, Grandma, you cried and cried;
Then Minnie, Wilma, Lois, Junior;
Finally a name to honor Senior,
Who somewhere in there sired another;
At least one more by a black mother;
She wasn't a servant or slave or maid;
A neighbor, no less, but Grandpa paid;
Run out of the county by the KKK
Who didn't hang him by the head;
And the law protected Grandpa to lay;
To have his way in Grandma's bed.
Then Deborah Babette and Olive Wright
Who didn't make it their first night.
So many babies, so much pain;
So much labor for one little woman.
An easy-going husband, funny and kind
In his own way, making moonshine;
Drinking a little and selling more;
Happier than her, both dirt poor.
Such a big name at birth for anyone;
She married and added the name "Harrison."
Julia Ann Josephine Amelia Green,
What was it that you dared to dream?

Grandpa and Hell

My first funeral I don't forget;
I think I was eight;
But I remember it well;
Preacher Parker preached Grandpa straight to Hell.

What! My dear sweet Grandpa
With his crossed but twinkling eyes;
Never hurt a soul but Grandma
And the mother of his half-black child.

Preacher Parker didn't know all that,
But he knew enough;
Preached Grandpa straight to Hell
Because he wouldn't go to church.

Didn't know about the moonshine
Back in the woods;
Didn't know about the KKK
Running him off in their hoods.

Grandma went to church without Grandpa,
Missing from the amen corner.
Did he feel unworthy or superior
Or did he feel neither?

Grandpa was easy-going and jolly;
Prone to boot-legging and folly;
He fathered at least fifteen children;
He liked to tell funny jokes about preaching.

But Preacher Parker got Grandpa back
At Grandpa's funeral with his attack.
Who knows the truth? Who can tell?
But I don't think that Grandpa's in Hell.

Goin' in the Woods

—◦◉◦—

How I hated goin' in the woods;
Doin' number two, relieving nature;
Doin' your business and courser words;
Meant no toilet inside or outdoors.

Before we moved into the hollow,
The front of our outdoor toilet door
Was right in front of our dining room window;
Such a pleasant mealtime reminder.
On Thanksgiving Day when I was four,
We heard my teen brother hollerin' aplenty;
The wind had blown the toilet over,
With my brother goin' to the bathroom in it.

Then we moved to the mountain "holler"
Daddy found and loved for he was a hunter.
There he could make his very own rules,
One of them being we could go in the woods.
Daddy was a builder; he could build either;
But for quite a while he built neither;
No toilet indoors or outdoors when we got out of bed;
It mattered not that we would dread:
What if we squatted on a copperhead?
So when I was five for about a year,
We went in the woods and snakes did fear.
One day there were voices; who did we hear?
Boy Scouts were hiking in our woods so near.
They saw our piles of poop, those Scouts;
Of that I'm sure; I have no doubts.
I felt a child's helpless humiliation;
One of the Scouts was my two-indoor-baths cousin.

We were not alone in our goin' in the woods;

I don't mean we seven shat together;
Squatting down in all kinds of weather;
Others went in the woods in our neighborhoods.
I don't just mean the deer and bears and other creatures;
I mean some of our other neighbors;
Most had toilets; some indoor bath comforts;
But we were poorer than my aunts and uncles.

We were too poor to have a catalog from Sears,
So we would use what paper we could spare.
One time Daddy, in the dark, to his despair,
Reached in his pocket and used his last dollar.
Speaking of dark, now it seems senseless;
I think it's now called learned helplessness;
At night we made do with one thunder mug;
Why didn't we each have a lard can or old jug?

A boy who would be in my first-grade class
Family went in the woods to do their business.
My family would eventually all move away,
But he and his sisters would always stay.
Except he, like many boys my age, went to Vietnam;
But when he came back he never again left home;
Married a nice wife, built beside his mama's;
His three sisters' homes in a row, all of them neighbors.
His sons went off and got their degrees;
Now those woods are his family's retreat.
Their home, their comfort, their satisfaction;
A peaceful place where their happiness can happen.

Is it now better, speaking of happiness?
Or when we went in the woods and had much less?
I thought our other neighbors had it much worse;
There were eleven of them and seven of us.
They lived in a little two-bedroom house,
Plus a small room for a bath but no fixtures;
I don't know how they all managed to fit there;
Like me they seemed happy they had each other.

Now I see many with an over-sized house;
Four people, five bedrooms; some with five baths.
Someone I know, when he came back from Africa,
Said although they are poor they really seem happier.
While here at home I watch HGTV;
Most homes people have here are too expensive;
I hear "I can't live with those old appliances"
Or that laughed-at bath or those popcorn ceilings.
Yes, you can live with a kitchen like mine;
I happen to think that my kitchen is fine.
And I'm grateful for my out-of-date bath;
And I could live without the other one-and-a-half.
Some even must have a vacation home, too,
To get away from their first home; boo-hoo;
But let's not admit a desperate refugee;
Let's just think of me, me, me.

You can be poor in spirit and rich in wealth;
First, be grateful if you have good health;
And you're safe from harm and have enough goods;
There are worse things than goin' in the woods.

Playing in the Woods

The woods were my world
From fall to spring;
With freedom to explore
With my girl's imagination.
Why just fall to spring?
Snakes were the reason!
My daddy and brothers killed twenty
Copperheads clearing land for our garden.

The loveliest spot of all
Was in those woods in the fall;
Where I sat on rocks to dream
Beside a peaceful, lovely little stream.
In our own perfect park
We would play until dark;
A grapevine nature's swing
Until I saw the first snake in spring.

Laurel thickets were my home;
Limbs and leaves formed each room.
A handsome Indian my pretend boyfriend,
When the laurel was in bloom I dreamed a wedding.
Running ridges was inviting;
Seeing what's ahead so exciting.
I never found it boring
But downright exhilarating.

I was eight, my brother four
When we'd run out the door;
To the woods to play, so carefree;
We'd take our niece, she was three.
We'd be gone for hours,
A couple at least;

And no one had fears;
It was the nineteen fifties.

We didn't always wear socks and shoes,
Even when we were playing in the woods.
Daddy found my niece's socks by the creek one winter;
She was three when we were wading in the water.
My birthday when I turned nine I remember;
In the woods running ridges in January;
Feeling nothing in the woods to fear or worry;
Back to our warm home and Mother's spice cake aroma.

Fifty years later, a January day,
Back in the woods where I used to play.
It was strangely warm;
I didn't think of any harm.
Me, my grand-kids, that lovely day,
Their friend from school, several others.
When I heard a hiss, rattle, rustle.
I said, "I think I heard a rattlesnake!"
Walking swiftly, we hadn't seen
A large rattler near a rock, perhaps a den;
Something I would never dream;
A snake in the woods and it's not yet spring.
My niece's husband poked it with a stick;
It quickly crawled away toward a sofa-sized rock.
I quickly led the kids away, one with no shoes;
When we just wanted to be walking in the woods.

My grand-daughter loves the woods or a lake.
And, unlike me, she's not afraid of a snake.
She likes to sleep in the back yard in a hammock;
Tho' it's nowhere near a sofa-sized rock.
Unlike me, she's not afraid of drowning in a lake.
But, like me, she may go barefoot but also likes shoes.
At six she said, "I'm not afraid of a 'lil 'ol snake."
But, like me, she likes playing in the woods.

My Teachers at North Cove

Started first grade with Miss McBee;
So beautiful and blonde and nice to me.
So scared that year I wouldn't pass;
"Promoted to second grade" when I peeked in her desk.
Old maid Miss Hicks, that poor woman,
Trying to teach us naughty little humans.
We girls in the cloak room kissing a boy one day,
All over his head; he cried; he was gay.
Third grade was beautiful Mrs Letellier;
She was new to us, not from around here.
It was rumored her husband had worked on the bomb.
My daddy had helped build her nearby home.
She let me do art in the back of the room.
Fourth grade was Mrs Mary Butt Brown;
As I recall she would often frown;
Said God didn't mean for man to go to the moon;
Sometimes I thought she flew on a broom.
But now I look back and wonder why
She put up with Diane and me when we'd fight;
Down on the ground tearing into each other;
I was in a blind rage when I tore off her collar,
Because bully Diane had insulted my mother.
I don't remember being punished or getting in trouble.

Fifth grade was newly-wed Justine Good Woody.
She wanted us all to be goody-goody.
That year I read our family medical guide;
Learned how she got pregnant; she couldn't hide.
We weren't to speak, man she was strict;
She would punish us for moving our lips.
Sixth grade was Beverly Lonon Foster, my sister's friend;
They had played on the same basketball team.
She was pretty and fun; gave me an A plus;

53

Girls wanted to be her; boys had a big crush.
She made learning fun, a big relief,
As it often should be is my belief.
Sometimes we stayed too long at recess;
Loved when she said, "There are too many tests."
Her father owned a local store;
My best friend Marilyn's daddy owned another;
The stores were robbed, and I was so ashamed;
My brother Al a robber when the suspects were named.
Seventh grade was Mrs McAfee.
"Who's the smartest, Cheryl or Marilyn?"
After breaking my heart, asked Romeo Ervin;
Already telling girls that he loved them.
(In seventh grade he was already smoking.
Saw him the other day; he carries around oxygen.)
Eighth grade was Theodore Roosevelt Braswell;
Dear and devout; had us read the Bible;
A daily devotion was one of his rules
Until we had no more prayer in schools.
(After all, it was against the Constitution;
And, oddly, back then, we had segregation
And many mean rules in a so-called Christian nation.)

Then high school and many teachers;
A wonderful principal, Mr John Childers;
Our hero, a veteran of World War II;
His main rule the Golden Rule ("don't boo").
He also taught and when I sat in his class,
I thought it was special, that we were blessed.
He taught a wide variety—
English, French, math, history.
Peggy Lonon Smith could teach anything—
(And she was my distant cousin)
English, history, sewing, cooking.
Later Pat Harr, both gifted to me;
One went to Appalachian State, one East Tennessee.
Todd Woody taught science and coached ball;
Biology, health, physics, chemistry;
(That's how it is when a school is small.)

I learned a lot; I took them all.
He even taught me geometry;
So, when I took it in college it was a breeze.
He made me study, challenged me.
Douglas McKinney and Todd Woody were co-workers and friends;
Todd Woody a bachelor, Douglas McKinney married with children;
Mr McKinney, called "Prof," quoted great writers, taught history;
But a long life was not his destiny;
While teaching he was battling a heart condition;
He didn't live to finish raising his children;
To see his daughter become a principal or his son a physician;
Todd Woody and his widow ended up marrying.
In junior year another teacher very dear
Came to teach at our school and made us love Shakespeare;
How we loved Julia Horton Arnold;
I cried for days when she got a brain tumor.
Other high school teachers; I respected them all;
And at our North Cove graduation I got to tell them so.
Commencement meant out into the world we'd go.
I had the knowledge for college in the fall.

Daddy Drunk With Guns

It was Easter; I was four;
She said it was a headache as she cried.
But I had seen him pull her hair
When she told him she was with their sixth child.
Loaded our family in his panel truck;
Didn't wreck; glad for the luck;
Mother went along to stay near;
Afraid what he might do, living in fear.
My stomach in knots, him drunk in the car;
"I saw your daddy drunk at the store,"
Said a girl in first grade; I felt such shame;
Not my daddy but the alcohol I'd blame.

Daddy mixed guns and knives, whiskey, gin.
Once it was Daddy with two other men;
Lined three kids against our living room wall;
Did those damned drunks have sense at all?
But one a judge, one a lawyer, Daddy's "friends."
Only buddies when they were drinking.
One of my sisters and two brothers against the wall;
They threw knives between the children
And paid no consequences at all.
Not only that, the men peed on our living room wall.
Guess that's drunken logic when there's no toilet
In a poor house and you have wealth,
And you don't think of the children's health.
Then two shots at one's beard, using Daddy's gun.
They even said the f-word, those drunken fools,
In front of us children, none older than eleven.
Did they think they were being cool?
I'm sure my modest mother was quite embarrassed.
Anything about sex would make her blush.
And I'm sure she hated not protecting us.
But when Daddy was sober they'd have fun and fuss.

I was a baby in Mother's arms,
And I didn't remember like the older ones.
But I heard the story and wonder the harm.
Who hurt more? Mother or the daughters or the sons?
One son appeared for his first DUI,
One of Al's several over the years,
Before that damned judge, my father's "friend";
Judging my brother. Did he pay for his sin?
Mother walked to a neighbor, not to family next door;
Taking us children, we went to his store.
Where she called the sheriff;
Not that it made a difference.
Daddy's mama came the following day;
Sunny and happy, whistling and gay.
Wondering why we had missed church.
"Poor baby," she said, about Daddy's headache.

Daddy shooting toward my other sister as she runs to the car,
Where her little girls watch as she runs through the yard.
She must be a whore because she's getting a divorce;
And we women are supposed to be nice.
I'm beside him on our porch;
I'm eight and in terror I watch.
Her husband touched our other sister,
But mister drunk defends molesting mister.

Daddy fears he's gone too far;
He suddenly one Sunday decides to stop the car;
Turns around and heads to the Baptist church
That we just passed; it's a bit too much.
I look at Mother; she looks at me;
Through his thinking we can see;
I'm only eight but I see through his plan
To save his ass, to get religion.
(But my nieces' daddy took them, and in revenge,
Never let them come to our home again.
But what about his molesting?
For years we were silent about the whole thing.
Thankfully, Daddy was not guilty of that wrongdoing.)

It's not the church of Daddy's father and mother;
Of course, Daddy has to go to another.
Not the Methodist church; he must rebel;
And go to the church where they shout and yell.
Was that the one he called the "Claw Hammer Church?"
Or was it the Baptist "Cut Throat Church?"
Both had fights between members, pray tell;
And both say sinners will go to Hell.
"Like Elvis," they said, with his shaking hips;
"And those wearing tight blue jeans,"
Our preacher and others said with their lips.
I knew better; still don't see the sins.
But Daddy, who had laughed at preachers
And at his own son who thought of being one;
Would invite the preacher for Sunday dinner,
And Mother would fry the weekly chicken.
Of course, I was glad Daddy wasn't getting drunk;
Sloppy, mean, driving drunk as a skunk.
I must admit there was a bit more piety,
But the religion didn't last longer than the sobriety.
Soon one night I ran to the neighbor;
Drunk Daddy had a gun, threatening Mother.
I can't remember why I was alone
With Mother and Daddy, her begging and crying;
And no one had a phone, no 9-1-1.
I was so relieved when I walked back in our door
That Mother wasn't dead in a pool of blood on the floor.
Daddy backslid; we thought that he would;
Most often on Friday, soon after he got paid.
A weekend drunk, no money for more;
And our dry county had no ABC store.

I was sixteen and now I was driving;
But didn't think I could say no to a parent.
Drunk Daddy decided he wanted more;
Made me drive him to the bootleg store.
When we came back home I went to my room,
Just wanting to get away from him.
He had his gun, said he'd shoot my door down.

I ran out of my room, grabbed the gun in his hand.
I was in a rage, and it's a wonder
That no one got shot when it happened;
When my hand touched the trigger;
There's still a scar near my finger.
I had to be tough; I didn't stay mad;
And since no one got shot I was just glad;
I didn't whine, just blamed the moonshine;
But in class after that I burst out crying.

Be mad at your parent?
That's not Christian, a Ten Commandment;
And do unto others, the Golden Rule;
And as Elvis said, "Don't Be Cruel."

My daddy still pulling such stunts and him a grandpaw,
Until finally my brother laid down the law.
Said, "I won't come back with your grandson at all."
Guess that finally hit home and Daddy got too old.

Now I'll end with a prophetic story
About Daddy and my mother's brother;
About my uncle's new shoes he let Daddy try on.
Young man Daddy walked off with them on his feet not to return.
My uncle said nothing, for he was about the best man I've known;
And Daddy was drunk and he had a gun.

Aunt Pearl

Few more fun than my dear Aunt Pearl;
Married at fifteen when she was just a girl.
Guess Grandma and Grandpa felt some relief,
For she didn't always abide by their belief.
When she went away to high school
She had never lived so close to town.
Treated her friends, broke more than one rule;
Wiped out Grandpa's bank account.

Married a Democrat; turns out he was a rake;
Maybe a cause of the electroshocks she'd take.
Active in the party, maybe even fraud I read;
According to the paper might have voted for the dead.

She liked to come to our house to stay the night.
We kids loved to have her; never a dull moment.
But Daddy would get rather annoyed when
She'd get out of bed in the night and eat kraut.
In the middle of the night the house would be cold;
In my parents' wood stove the fire she would stoke.
Then she'd sit in front of the open stove door
To get herself warm while the house filled with smoke.

Once when she came for more than a day,
She told my parents she had to get away.
Uncle Milt was wanting her to have sex;
They were in their seventies; what would it be next?
He took her to a movie she thought was "My Fair Lady";
Knowing him, it was no mistake; it was "My Bare Lady."
Her son wrote about that in the Charlotte Observer;
He mostly covered NASCAR and his father and mother.

Aunt Pearl's daughter lived in Washington,

And she'd sometimes go to DC to visit.
And during the televised Watergate hearing
She sure didn't like Nixon and didn't want to miss it.
One day there was a ruckus we saw on TV;
Apparently, Aunt Pearl didn't like the questions;
Did Senator Sam say, "Now, Pearl if you don't hush
I'll have to ask you to leave"?
When she came back from Washington
I went with my husband to meet her train;
I teasingly asked her if she caused the ruckus;
She coyly answered that she wore her red, white and blue dress.
My husband lifted her two heavy bags;
"What you got in here, rocks?" he asked.
"Yes, I took them to the Smithsonian to be tested";
As if that was the most natural thing ever said.
Turns out she might have been onto something,
For in her particular part of the country;
In the mountains of western North Carolina
Are minerals used in the world's computers.

Aunt Pearl was an artist, painted murals on her walls;
Did taxes and taught art in schools.
She could crochet and knit and sing songs that she wrote.
And vote for those who couldn't vote?
She liked to fish while she'd sneak and smoke;
And she liked to cook fish when she was able.
She wasn't crazy about doing housework;
Not really nasty, but let her cat on the kitchen table.

Daddy had been dealing with her for more years than me;
And we really didn't know much about ECT.
She'd been in and out of the state mental hospital;
Laughed and said next time maybe she'd try jail.
We loved her, and being bipolar is not a joke;
And among bipolars are special folk.
There were ups and downs with my dear Aunt Pearl;
But bipolars sure make a less dull world.

Aunts and Uncles

I guess every family has their characters;
Some maybe more than their share.
So there are lots of stories of ours
About our aunts and uncles.
I devoted one poem to Aunt Pearl alone,
And I hope you read it before you are done.
For she was by far the most fun,
But some of the others were also interesting.

When Mamie and Ike were first lady and president
I had an uncle Ike and aunt Mamie of my own.
She shot him in the belly; then they were done;
Maybe not a good idea to marry your first cousin.
Uncle Ike lived but not again with Aunt Mamie;
I'm sure some problems were due to his drinking.
We kids would say, "Show us your belly button";
Now on his side, due to his fiery first cousin;
To us kids Uncle Ike would always comply,
When "Show us your belly button" to him we'd cry;
But in court one day, where it really counts,
He slapped an attorney and was charged with contempt.
Uncle Ike didn't divorce Mamie for many years;
Long after her started living with "Aunt" Lucille.
When Uncle Ike and "Aunt" Lucille would come to spend the night,
Mother made me sleep with her, and my brother with Uncle Ike.
You see, divorce back then was considered a sin;
In the early 1950s things were different then.

When writing about Daddy I already told how he rebelled;
When the bald preacher came for Sunday dinner;
While the grown-ups ate first; and then the children,
Boys Ike and Hub (Daddy) shaved their naughty heads.
Uncle Leonard, like Daddy, wouldn't go to church with his wife

Until their boyhood church got its first female preacher;
Daddy and Uncle Leonard went back to church
once to laugh at such a creature.
And when a cult moved close by, called "The
Way, The Truth, and The Life,"
Some burned a cross in their yard, and Uncle Leonard shot their sign.

In high school I feared I'd have to work harder,
When my history teacher said that my Uncle Earl
Had been his boss on the railroad and a real slave driver;
But said he wouldn't ask him to do what he wouldn't do first.

I've told how Uncle Lloyd fought in World War II;
Wounded twice, it's a miracle he came through;
With two Purple Hearts he came back a hero;
Some said he later sold guns to Fidel Castro.
He was a good-looking charmer and got his way
When he took away rich Henry Belk's beautiful fiancee.
Maybe one of the biggest mistakes a young woman would make,
For handsome hero Uncle Lloyd was also a rake.

Aunt Bertie liked to buy and fix houses for profit;
Told me she could turn a quarter into a dollar.
When she got old she said she owned Florida,
And thought she was the boss of her nursing home doctor.

Uncle Jack nice with success, not as wild for some reason;
Raised four fine sons, one with two gold records;
One played football for Duke, one golfed for Davidson;
One Carolina track, one quarterback and athletic director.
(Yes, cousin John Swofford is the ACC Commissioner.)

Now to my mother's side:
Half of her siblings were young when they died,
But I'll write some of those who survived.
Uncle Walter I never knew, but Mother spoke of him often;
She said he was full of life and very handsome;
He was in the Army when he died of car wreck injuries;
And from three states at his funeral were three fiancees.

63

My Uncle EL was handsome and funny too.
But how could he have been such a fool?
Told me Coretta Scott King was married to JFK.
Afraid he heard that at a meeting of the KKK.
Aunt Wilma our county's first in the Women's Auxiliary Corps;
Yes, she joined the Army in the second World War;
Trained as a medic but didn't go to war.
Many of the women didn't have to go as far.
We'd love it when she'd send mother a letter;
She seemed to always have a funny story;
Threw her first wedding ring from a bus into the Missouri;
Funny she then married a tall-tales-telling Storie.
Aunt Minnie was a sweet, humble woman,
But when I was a kid I feared she'd feed me poison
Because she and mother had a fuss one day.
"You pet [me] more than [my sister]," she would say.
She served food in our school lunch room,
So, I thought poison might be my doom.
Uncle Spencer a wise, smart, humble man;
Don't know how anyone could not love him;
He'd always have us an RC Cola and a Moon Pie;
Did what he had to do with a pleasant smile.
Something happened to troubled Aunt Nell;
I don't know what; it's really hard to tell.
She'd send mean letters to my good mother,
Saying she should go to church and hear her preacher.

When one aunt got older she seemed in competition
To live longer than any other sibling.
My mother outlived all of hers; only one of Daddy's lived as long.
When Aunt Nell died, my daughter said,
"Congratulations, Granny! You won!"

Brothers and Sisters

How do some sisters and brothers
Come from the same fathers and mothers?
Some insult and argue and fuss and fight,
And won't admit who is wrong or right.

They gossip and ridicule and stab in the back.
They speak against you and lies at that;
They judge each other in court and out,
While thinking their own crimes don't count.

Some go to church, even teach a class;
Pretending to be righteous and pious.
"All non-believers should burn in Hell."
But what about you sinners, pray tell?

"You can't go to Heaven if you're gay";
Say some who had affairs and married multiply.
Some won't talk; some won't listen;
Might that not also be a sin?

Some took to Trump; to Hillary some took;
Which divides even more and adds to the hate;
Now some even unfriending on Facebook;
Sometimes I wonder if it's too late.

They could be good friends, not enemies;
They could show more love, not much less;
Each may be better or worse, one way or others;
Everyone matters and hurts, sisters and brothers.

They could value more their history,
For some can no longer tell their story.
They can cry and laugh about their past,
But it's too sad if their bond doesn't last.

65

Family a Suicide Squad?

First, I will say there's too much shame,
And families are not always to blame.
But it hit me last night while watching TV
That a suicide squad is sometimes your family.

"You're too fat; you need to lose weight.
You can't eat that; it's already too late."
Or "You're too skinny; you need to eat more.
You're no bigger than a poot"; or You're a bore."

When you tried playing ball you were ridiculed;
Schools can have suicide squads, too.
You won't be a cheerleader or play a sport;
So you watch others and from the stands you root.

Your daddy hates your sister; you hate your mother.
Your daddy pets you; she pets your brother.
There may be sibling rivalry from the time you're born;
And then more damage when a family is torn.

Coming out as LGBT,
When you certainly need your family;
Some turn on you as if you're bad;
Say your love is wrong; it makes you sad.

You may be agnostic or atheist, your family religious;
They may be conservative; you a liberal activist;
You may be for civil rights; they may be racist;
You may be against banning all Muslims; they may be bigots.

Some return from war with PTSD;
If you don't have it you're quite lucky.
Family may not be at all at fault,
But do some give enough support?

You may be this; you may be that;
Too smart, too dumb, no telling what.
You may choose other choices,
And hear disappointment in your family voices.

Some turn to drugs; some overdose;
Then some families may treat them worse;
At a time when they may need help most;
That's a time when many get more lost.

Some families among the worst
Who abuse, ignore, neglect, molest;
Even some we think are the best
Are secret suicide squads no less.

The father often gone, some mothers too;
With or without, try to muddle through.
Sometimes one's best is not good enough;
You try and try but life is rough.

You're not alone in your private Hell;
We don't know how others feel.
Like beautiful Marilyn Monroe,
Adored by all, a president and Joe DiMaggio.
Lincoln, too, suffered depression,
Not just due to the war situation;
So did Martin Luther King,
As a boy and surely as a man,
And many another known or not known.

Try to be strong, try to be tough;
Try to be kind; be good enough;
Try to overcome; see your worth;
A suicide squad don't join or succumb.

Where Did This Happen?

—⊷◉⊶—

Where did this bad treatment happen?
Men getting away with abuse and harassment?
Of women and girls and sometimes boys;
And sometimes men on men in prison;
Treating them as if they are their sex toys?
Or not letting women vote or drive a car,
Or go to school or be priests or go very far?

Was it in Afghanistan by the Taliban?
Or in Saudi Arabia or Iraq or Iran?
Or by followers of Bin Laden and in Pakistan?
Or was it in Charleston and Galveston and Washington?

They call her a "whore," the fallen woman;
Families can treat them like they're not human.
In some places fallen women are stoned to death;
Yes, hit with stones until they take their last breath.
Some are driven to take their own life
When they no longer want to be a wife.
"If you will shoot yourself, I'll send you a gun";
Said a father to a mother suffering depression.
"I'll cause you to lose your job and break you;
The money I would get would be worth more than you."
Driving a woman to a suicide attempt;
It may only get worse, with more contempt.
"Your husband should have shot you";
Not caring what she's going through.
Some become even more angry and mean;
Driving a person to try to end it again.
"You might as well kill yourself"; so cruel;
Say the so-called religious, breaking the Golden Rule.

They can't always turn to their families with women,
When a mother sighs and says "Men take up for men";
Like the mother who said one of the worst things I'd ever hear:
"I wish she'd try to kill herself in Florida; I've never been there."

"Divorce is a sin," not just said by a Roman Christian,
Or a Buddhist, a Hindu, a Jew, a Muslim or Protestant,
While sinning against boys and girls and men and women.
And some men are even heard laughing and bragging
About how they have gotten away with their grabbing;
Yet they're not stoned; some even thrive;
When many victims of abuse hardly survive.
Where in the world do such things happen?
All over the world, in China, India and Japan;
By Americans, Germans, Nigerians, Russians,
And some others claiming to defend their religions.

He Drank Himself to Death

—◦✦◦—

He once looked like a movie star,
Had his own business; he could have gone far.
Perfect smile, tall, dark and handsome;
He came a long way from where he had come,
And drank himself to death when he was 31.
He was six years old and sleeping with his daddy
When he awoke to find his daddy dead.
He was the youngest of ten when his mama widowed.
They were destitute, times were lean.
He was smart and could quickly learn,
But he didn't get much formal education.
When he was seventeen he became a Marine;
I think that's when he started drinking.
But he soon got out and would serve no longer
When he accidentally shot himself in the shoulder.
He married my sister when he was nineteen;
Swept her off her feet, she was sixteen.
My sister was also a seductive beauty;
They would have a precious girl and boy.
They worked hard and bought a nice home;
They lived for awhile near Washington.
He was very proud he supervised pavers
Who paved the entrance to Camp David.
He formed his own paving business,
And could have been on the road to success.
But he drank more and more alcohol,
And it began to take its toll.
He fulfilled all four items of the CAGE questionnaire;
The alcohol now had the power.
He knew he needed to cut down;
When people criticized his drinking he was annoyed;
And, of course he felt guilty he was letting people down;
But he still wanted a drink when his eyes opened.

70

He said he'd rather die than do without it;
Famous last words of a dying addict.

So sad how a substance can take hold,
Whether it's other drugs or alcohol;
And go against all that you're told;
Wish it was as simple as "Just say no."
A psychology professor, himself an alcoholic,
Told me alcoholism stems from feeling inadequate.
He blamed his father in part because he said,
When my professor's brother died as a lad,
He wished he (my professor-to-be) was dead instead.
So you can be an alcoholic without a GED
Or be an alcoholic with a Harvard PhD.

My sister's husband went into a downward spiral,
And they were on their way to getting a divorce.
He was living alone with much despair,
And died like Nicholas Cage in Leaving Las Vegas.
Somehow what killed him made him feel more alive;
Down when he didn't have it; with it full of life;
Fun with it, the life of the party or at a bar;
Withdrawn without it; he'd go sit in his car;
My sister's husband was like my own brother;
Married to his nephew, I would soon become a mother.
When my sister's husband died I cried and cried;
I could only think of my little nephew and niece;
How they no longer had a daddy, not his peace;
But at least one said he might be the father of my child.
To set the record straight that is wrong and mean;
Sure, he was handsome just like my ex-husband;
Who is definitely the father of both my children;
Never did I touch or lust for my sister's husband.

Old White Woman

Something I totally didn't foresee
Was how discrimination might be used against me.
I've been an activist for civil rights;
I thought I understood most of the fights.
When I lived in Atlanta about a decade ago,
I started to feel something I didn't before know;
I started to feel like a minority;
And why not? I guess some would agree.

I interviewed for a job at a university,
And felt I was being treated like a minority.
The job interviewer was a male, a Jew;
He was the women's boss, the department head;
I saw only one other white person, not even a few;
And no one with gray hairs like mine on their head.
I was as qualified for the job as anyone;
The job was to replace the only white woman;
Although I was a good, qualified worker, I wasn't hired;
I had great passion for the work, and I didn't get tired;
A black woman I knew with much less qualification
Got hired in that department. Was it discrimination?
Was it because I was white or old?
Or because of neither or both, truth be told?

I got many comments at work when I decided to go gray,
By black women in the office who would often say,
"When are you going to do something about your hair?"
By the way, they never asked about my son away at war.

I've been told the problem was my over-qualification;
Isn't that another bad form of discrimination?
I've interviewed from Atlanta to Washington;
Paying for all the costs of my transportation;

Yet, when I worked in HR I saw many men
Get checks for their trips; I get frustration.
I've only gotten paid for my interview expenses once.
I thought when I moved back home I'd have a better chance.
Over a hundred jobs; I applied and applied;
Not hired; I'm told, "You're over-qualified."
My former boss said she gave me a good reference
The few times she got a call to ask about me.
We got along well, so what made the difference?
I don't think it's that hard to see;
I'm pretty sure now it's because of my age;
It still doesn't mean it's not a reason for rage.
We're still people; we may like to dance life's dance;
We may like equal rights, to still have a chance.
Guess if we live long enough we adapt to aging;
But it doesn't mean we shouldn't still be raging
About injustice in many forms, for civil rights;
Trying to keep fighting all the good fights.

Ellen Not of Troy

We thought her uppity, our local Miss Ellen;
Descendant of leaders of our land.
You'd think she thought she was Troy's own Helen,
Who fell off Mt Ida with her wedding band.

"You'll likely marry the first sawed-off man"
Who asks you to marry, to take his hand;
To offer you a wedding band;
Said Miss Ellen with her own sawed-off man.

And that we did like many others,
And some became unwilling mothers.
Now with children hand in hand,
No longer feeling for our man.

Some of us stayed, some of us went,
Giving all 'til all was spent.
Some got another good or bad man;
Took his hand, his wedding band.

Miss Ellen stayed with her sawed-off husband.
Did she wonder what she might have been?
Could she have been a leader of our land?
But she fell off Mt Ida with her wedding band.

Why Should Not Old Women Be Mad?*

WHY should not old women be mad?
Some have known a likely Ms
Who had a sound writer's wrist
Lose to an awful narcissist.
A girl who learned David and Darwin once,
Live to bear children to a dunce;
Or a Cheryl of social welfare dream,
Stand in front of the courthouse to scream.
Some women think it a matter of right
That against injustice we should fight.
None should starve; don't leave to chance;
Help those who can't help themselves advance.
Life is not like a lighted screen;
No single story will we find
Of an unbroken, happy mind,
Or a finish worthy of the work;
Some know nothing of this sort.
Observant old women know it well;
And when they know what old books tell;
Let's write better books; they can be had;
Know why an old woman should be mad.

*Adapted from "Why Should Not Old Men Be Mad" by William Butler Yeats
[Yeats died in 1939, over 70 years ago; it is this author's understanding that
per EU/UK law his works are now in the public domain]

Leonardo da Vinci

An intriguing Italian Renaissance man;
Born near Florence, Italy in the area of Vinci
Of a notary and unmarried peasant woman;
But related to the powerful family de'Medici.
Some say he's the greatest painter ever;
Perhaps best known for The Last Supper;
Also The Mona Lisa and The Vitruvian Man;
Many other paintings like Lady With An Ermine.
Seems something in the water in Italy
Around the time of the 15th century.
Michelangelo from Florence, Raphael from Urbino;
Christopher Columbus from Genoa
Became one of the most famous explorers;
Amerigo Vespucci from Florence, also;
All were Leonardo da Vinci contemporaries.
Though he painted The Last Supper and Christ and his mother,
Leonardo wasn't otherwise into all the religious fervor;
He lived away from Florence during Savonarola's "reign of terror"
When there were "bonfires of the vanities" when theocracy took over.
Da Vinci a polymath with many interests;
Very curious and drew significant sketches.
He drew sketches of structures and flying machines
And parachutes and tanks long before they were inventions.
In more ways than one, a man ahead of his times.
He had many ideas but didn't publish his findings.
His curiosity about cadavers about more than art;
To medical science he added his part.
A wide range of subjects filled his mind;
Anatomy and physiology, botany, geology,
Literature, writing, maps and cartography;
Math, music, astronomy, architecture,
History, physics, other science, even sculpture;
But not asked, as far as known, to do the Sistine Chapel.

Personally mysterious but professionally well-known;
He never married; don't know if he lived alone.
At age 24 he and three other young men
Were charged with sodomy but the case dismissed.
A vegetarian known to buy caged birds he released.
In his early 60s he lived in the Vatican in Rome,
Where Raphael and Michelangelo were also working.
He saw Pope Leo X and King Francis I at a meeting;
Then from Rome, France would be his last home.
Friends can ask friends to do some things strange and silly,
Like Leonoardo da Vinci's friend, the king of France;
Who commissioned Leonardo to make a mechanical lion
That could walk and show a chest full of lilies.
Da Vinci died in France in 1519 at age 67.

*Source mainly Wikipedia, obtained July 25, 2017

Sir Isaac Newton

———⁃◦⊙◦⁃———

Newton was born in 1642 in Lincolnshire, England,
(On Christmas Day, I guess another gift to the world)
In a hamlet three months after his father died.
When he was three his mother remarried;
It was told he was mad at his mother;
For marrying his hated step-father;
So, he mostly lived with his maternal grandmother;
And boy Isaac threatened to burn down his mother's home;
Don't know whether or not he atoned.
Newton's not the first in my reading I've found
To lose a father before he was born;
Who went on to have great success;
Were they made stronger by the stress?
Newton went to Trinity College of Cambridge as a young man;
When he got his BA he wasn't thought distinguishing.
Cambridge closed for two years due to the Great Plague,
So, he had to wait to work on his master's degree.
During that time he developed theories on calculus;
And colors and optics and laws of gravitation;
And Newton's famous three laws of motion:
One, an object at rest will remain at rest, inertia;
Two, force equals mass times acceleration;
Three, for every action there is an equal and opposite reaction;
Since then the unit for force is called a "newton."
He tried to get back into Cambridge for more education.
He had read the Bible and had some religion,
But a controversy because he varied from convention;
Something about his views on the Church of England;
But he got in when King Charles II gave him permission.
Newton would come to be recognized
As one of the smartest people ever alive;
The first calculation of the speed of sound to theorize;
And the mathematics of acceleration to realize.

He helped remove all doubts about the solar system;
The Earth's not at the center; how foolish of them;
Studying the tides and equinoxes and that the Earth is round;
Studied astronomy and wrote Opticks about the things he found;
Advancing man's knowledge, he'd work and hope;
And developed the first reflecting telescope.
He's credited with classical mechanics and much in physics;
And his main work Principia: Mathematics Principles.
Newton interested in chemistry; then it was alchemy.
Keynes said that Newton not the first in the Age of Reason;
But for some reason said he was the last magician;
Even though he is credited with the binomial theorem;
And Newton might have developed calculus independently;
But that's also a matter of controversy;
Some say Newton AND Leibniz, some disagree.

Newton was knighted by Queen Anne of England;
And was twice a brief time a member of Parliament;
And became President of the Royal Society,
Where today Stephen Hawking is one of the scientists.

Newton never married but had a four-year friend;
A Swiss man, intense, a fellow mathematician;
Newton in his forties when the friendship would end;
And Newton would suffer a nervous breakdown;
Newton died in his sleep, at age 84, perhaps a virgin.

I think I learned the binomial theorem, but wanted to curse
Newton and much of the math in my calculus course;
Actually, I took four terms of calculus and made two A's
But never used it since; what a big waste.
Don't get me wrong; I love education;
And it's always needed in every nation;
A good education makes a good foundation.
And whether you need to know calculus or not;
It's important to know about Sir Isaac Newton.

*Source mainly Wikipedia, obtained July 25, 2017

Meeting Jimmy Carter

It was sometime around 1990,
When I worked for Emory University Psychiatry.
I went to see him talk at his presidential library.
He talked of the great work of the Carter Center;
Of ending blindness from a parasite that lives in the river;
Of ending worms that can grow through the skin and can cripple.
Then after the talk he mingled with us,
Including a group of international students.
I was in awe when he stopped and stood
And talked with just me and two others.

President Carter would sometimes teach an Emory class
Beside my daughter's classroom; even she was impressed.
I would see President Carter twice again,
The second time at the 1992 Emory commencement.
He introduced Mikhail Gorbachev, the guest speaker.
Wow! President Carter and the last USSR leader.
Two heroes of the world to people like me;
Guess no greater two people would I ever see.

The last time I saw Jimmy Carter in person
Was at a bookstore in Atlanta at a book signing.
I was wearing high heels for no good reason;
Bought his book Talking Peace for him to sign.
After working all day, two hours I waited in line;
And when I got up to President Carter's table,
He didn't look up, but he started to giggle.
Behind President Carter stood a pretty young blonde.
He was about seventy, and my book he signed.
I was still getting wolf whistles back in the day,
But President Carter didn't give me any looks.
Did I really hear him to the young blonde woman say,
"With you standing behind me, I don't know if I can sign these books."

You'd think that he would have learned a lesson,
When about fifteen years before he was running for president;
And such silliness almost caused him to lose,
When he said he lusted in his heart in a Playboy interview.

I guess this just shows that we're all human;
And President Carter's greatness he has more than proven.
His work for the poor, the sick, for women,
And writing more great books I'm still reading.

I've also met President Carter's wife Rosalynn,
When I worked a couple of years at her mental health symposium.
She was gracious and nice, what you'd expect of his wife.
Both so deserving of a good, long life.
Jimmy and Rosalynn Carter have made a great team.
They don't make anyone feel they are better than them.
The thing about the Carters, they are kind and caring,
Showing what it's like to be a good American.
I would likely have seen the Carters again,
But I moved from Atlanta and haven't had the occasion.

Meeting Ted Turner

I walked in the door at Ted's Montana Grill.
Ted was there; I had no idea.
Near my job at an Atlanta hospital;
Went only to go have a good meal.
Everyone knew him, his reputation;
How he was never husband of the year,
But he gave the first big check to the Carter Center;
How he pledged a billion dollars to the United Nations.
Knew he owned the Braves, from worst to first
In their league, on to the World Series.
Knew he was called Captain Outrageous;
Where others died he won the race;
He was courageous, the storm was rough;
Knew he's not like the rest of us.
Owning Turner Classic Movies
Like great "Gone with the Wind"
And "Dr Zhivago" and "Treasure Island."
(I saw "The Misfits" on TCM not long ago,
The last film for Clark Gable and Marilyn Monroe.)
"I will have world news!" started CNN;
(He said to no longer use the word "foreign")
Still going strong even without him.
Suddenly he walks out of the men's room;
I'm in shock, about to swoon.
He's meeting customers like a Walmart greeter;
Friendly and fun; what could be neater?

We started to talk as I often do,
And he seemed to like to talk, too.
I told him how when I moved to Atlanta,
I wanted to meet him, maybe marry him, too.
When I heard he'd married Jane Fonda,
I said, "Darn!" And I was so blue.

Mattie-at-my-work's mother, his maid, had an in;
And I was fool enough to be believing
I could meet him; and at forty, I could tame that man;
And he wouldn't take up with other women.
Told him I worked at Emory when a doctor
I knew Ted knew became department head.
I said "I know" when Ted loudly said,
"He's my psychiatrist!" (as many have read)

The MLK Day Parade*

Dick Gregory's death the other day
Brought back memories of the time I marched,
On January 21, 1992, in the MLK Day parade.
The cold wind whipped all around; my face got chapped.
I marched with the local National Organization for Women,
Between a Gay Pride group and a group of Iranians.

Seems we started on Peachtree Street; ended on Auburn Avenue in Atlanta.
We walked by the Fox Theater where ten-year-old King
Sang in the church choir in 1939 at the premier of Gone with the Wind.
I didn't even realize who was marching in front;
(I do remember that I wore a long red coat);
Turns out it was Coretta Scott King, and
Winnie Mandela from South Africa.

The parade ended at a stage set up for the event
At the Martin Luther King Jr Historic District;
Where King Jr was born and baptized and buried;
Where his daddy was preacher, and he co-preached;
And where his mother Alberta was church organist at Ebenezer Baptist;
Not far from Booker T Washington high school where King had studied;
Or from Morehouse College where he entered at fifteen and graduated.

Six years after King Jr was killed at age 39
At Ebenezer Baptist Church there was another awful crime.
His mother was shot on Sunday morning playing the organ.
How can people take so much mourning?
Two others were wounded; she and a deacon died;
I can't even imagine how so many must have cried.
A young crazed black man from Ohio named Marcus didn't get far;
He seemed delirious when he kept saying it was because of the war.
(I guess he meant Vietnam; it was 1974.
Or could it have been the Civil War?

84

After all, look at current events;
But none of it really makes sense.)
Alberta was shot about a hundred yards from her son Martin's tomb.
Some parades some years have had the threat of a bomb.
How can some people be so damned mean to them?

As we got to the end of the parade that day,
I heard a familiar voice coming from the stage.
It was Kris Kristofferson's, the master of ceremonies;
Actor, singer, song-writer who won a Golden Globe and Grammys;
On stage with Coretta and Winnie were Maxine Waters,
And Dick Gregory and others I can't remember.
Winnie Mandela spoke with much power and vigor.
Dick Gregory joked something about people
Who were white and pink and red and tan,
For some reason calling him a colored man.
I won't add much about Martin Luther King Jr or Nelson Mandela;
Volumes have been written that can tell it better;
But they were two great and mighty leaders;
Like too many, Mandela imprisoned; King, too, among martyrs.
Still going strong at 79 in Congress is Maxine Waters.

*Some details from Wikipedia, obtained August 22, 2017

Trail of Tears

I grew up going to Cherokee,
A tourist attraction to our family;
Pictures with "Indians" beside a tepee;
At school a lot about it no one taught me.

We didn't learn of the injustice
To those who owned this land before us.
I had no idea, not one iota
About the Cherokee capital at New Echota.
New Echota had better homes than ours
More than a hundred years later;
But tragedy to come that could hardly be greater.
New Echota had an upper court, a lower court;
They even had a printing press.
Could it be some were jealous?
So unfair to this native and part-mixed race.
A thriving place, the Cherokee nation;
Never dreaming the hard-ships they were facing.
The Cherokees led by Chief John Ross,
Who'd lose his wife, would face great loss.

Gold found in the mountains
Of Georgia and the Carolinas.
Time for the whites to take the land
Of the largely native Cherokee band.
Once in battle leader Junaluska
Had saved the life of Andrew Jackson;
Then when Jackson became president,
Junaluska went to him to beg for mercy.
Jackson's order to remove the Cherokee
Was carried out in "the land of the free...
The home of the brave," of "liberty";
The land of lies, it seems to me.

To stockades they went from summer to fall;
Forced from their homes, Chief Ross and all;
On a cold October morning with drizzling rain;
Many on foot, thousands by wagon.
All leaving their homes against their wills;
Some of them escaped to the hills;
To what would become the east Cherokee reservation
Where I toured as a child the Cherokee nation.
Broken arrows, broken spirits.
Broken hearts, broken treaties;
Disease and exposure; lack of human loyalty;
While the privileged are treated like royalty.
Leaving their homes to suffer their fate,
Many forced to Oklahoma the cold winter of 1838.
A young widow died with a papoose on her back;
And two small children holding her hand;
Too weak to walk, she sank to the ground;
But compassion for her some would lack;
And some say, "God doesn't put more on you than you can stand."

Along the Trail of Tears those awful days,
Maybe four thousand unmarked graves;
Chief Ross's wife, the young widow, many others
Of our nation's Cherokee sisters and brothers.

*Mainly from the booklet "Cherokee Legends and the Trail of Tears," adapted
by Thomas Bryan Underwood. Cherokee Publications, Cherokee NC, 1956,
2002.

Andrew Jackson

Something I never thought I'd do
Was write a poem about this Andrew.
Mad at him for the Trail of Tears;
I didn't know about all his tears.
Born in 1767 in Waxhaws in Carolina
A couple of years after his parents came from Ireland;
Maybe to Philadelphia, then across the Appalachians;
Born three weeks after his father killed in an accident.

Too young to fight in the Revolutionary War,
He with brother Robert became a militia courier.
He was thirteen and had been about eleven
When after a battle his brother Hugh died of heat exhaustion.
He and Robert were captured in January when he was nearly fourteen.
An officer slashed him with a sword on his face and hand
When he refused to polish the British officer's boots.
His hatred toward the British would have deep roots.
Both boys got smallpox in prison and nearly starved to death.
A few months later in April their mother got them released.
Nursed her sons but Robert died in three days and Andrew got stronger;
Then she nursed other POWs on two ships in Charleston harbor;
Until, like many on the ships, she died of cholera in November.

Few have risen quite so fast and far.
Andrew studied law and by age twenty qualified for the bar.
At twenty-one moved to Nashville and bought his first slave;
A regrettable, wrong practice other presidents would have.
Was Tennessee Attorney General by age twenty-four.
Jackson kept climbing higher and higher.

Served in the US Congress, the House and Senate;
Before he was thirty the Tennessee constitutional convention.

At thirty-four named Commander of the Tennessee militia,
While also a justice on the Tennessee Supreme Court.
Besides his years as military battle commander,
In more than one duel he was a partner.
One left him with a musket ball in his lung near his heart;
It would remain causing pain nearly forty years 'til he'd part.

Most my age have heard one of Johnny Horton's catchy songs
About Colonel Jackson fighting the British in New Orleans.*
Jackson also fought the Indians and Spanish over Florida;
And in 1821 he would briefly be Florida's governor.
He went back to the US Senate three years later.
I guess Old Hickory thought his fighting was over.

Then his presidential campaign became a free-for-all;
It's hard to believe all the names they would call.
He opposed John Quincy Adams, fighting for a second term;
Oh, the things that were said by both sides to cause harm.
Jackson's mother called a whore, his father called a mulatto,
As if there was something wrong with being part Negro.
Adams' famous folks were considered high class,
While Jackson was made out to be white trash.
And Andrew's wife Rachel had a past;
Her marriage before Andrew did not last.
A divorce was a disgrace back in those days,
And she was called a bigamist.
Adam's people may have been meanest;
They even claimed that Jackson cannibalized Indians.
But Jackson's people played dirty pool, too;
Said the people paid for Adams' billiard table in a White House room.
And what would a campaign be without Russia?
Jackson's people said Adams when Russian Minister afar
Got a girl to be a prostitute for the Russian Czar!
(But nothing known about a golden shower;
I just couldn't help but stick that in there.)
Jackson defeated Adams but at great cost;
Rachel died of a heart attack before he took office.

Andrew buried Rachel on Christmas Eve;
Over and over he would deeply grieve.
He would blame his opponents until the world he'd leave.

Jackson served eight years with grief on his mind;
Still fighting battles but of another kind;
A man Jackson fired struck him one day;
Though chased by Washington Irving the man got away.
Jackson the first US president someone tried to kill;
He was outside the Capitol on Capitol Hill;
A man pulled out a pistol but it misfired;
He pulled out another and it, too, misfired.
Jackson hit the man with his cane, not a shrinking violet;
The would-be assassin was caught by Davy Crockett.
The two pistols retested by government officials;
Pistols fired perfectly; some said divine providence.

The Indians still a problem; so were Texas and Mexico;
Davy Crockett lost Congress and died at the Alamo.
Slavery always a problem and on the nation's conscience;
Where in Hell was that damned divine providence?
The National Bank, the economy, people out of work;
Said to be the only president who paid off the national debt.
Just before he turned seventy he left office;
Lived to be seventy-eight; man, was he tough!
He died with heart failure, a musket ball in his lung, and tuberculosis.

Andrew who was orphaned when he was fourteen;
As far as we know never by nature fathered children;
But with his wife Rachel they became parents and guardians
Of eight orphaned children of family and friends;
Plus three adopted sons, Rachel's nephew Andrew
Jr, and two orphaned Indians.
After learning more of Jackson, I now feel shame;
I judged only perhaps the worst of him;
For good and bad he was to blame.
He could have not had slaves all those years,

And he could have stopped the Trail of Tears;
But some even claim it helped save lives;
Like Hiroshima and Nagasaki some rationalize.
The more I learn the more I know it's hard
To know when and how to start and stop war;
To know which side of the fight to fight
To always be on the side of right.

*Song "The Battle of New Orleans"
Source for most of poem is Wikipedia, obtained July 11, 2017

The Golden Rule

Religion, besmidgeon;
What's the big fuss?
When the Golden Rule
Is what's good for us.
Not do to others as they do to you,
But as you'd have them do to you.

So many -isms, so much iniquity;
Agnosticism, Atheism, Buddhism, Christianity;
So many beliefs among humanity;
Hedonism, Hinduism, Humanism,
Islam, Jainism, Judaism,
Sikhism, Taoism, Zoroastrianism, others;
It's how we treat our sisters and brothers.

Capitalism, communism, fascism,
Libertarianism, socialism, scientism;
Over 200 -isms, the list is long;
But are any of them all right or all wrong?

All the teachings, philosophy and such,
Really don't count for much
Lest you use the Golden Rule.
All the science, all the thought;
Power and wealth count for naught
Lest you use the Golden Rule.

I Feel the World Crying

I feel the world crying
In need while we are buying
Things we don't need.
Too much apathy and greed.

I feel the world's pain;
Too many for self-gain.
Many could be more aware;
How can so many not care?

I've ached for too many years
For all the pain, grief, and fears.
I feel I've cried oceans,
Until I have no more tears.

Earth Days

I remember what was called the first Earth Day;
I was in college April 22, 1970;
But we've really known always;
All days should be Earth days.

I'm glad there was an industrial revolution,
So with much of the world I'm in collusion.
But when was it ever the right solution
To not pay attention to all the pollution?
We all enjoy electrical power,
While coal smoke and smog dirty our air.
And who would give up driving a car,
Tho' the car fumes fill the atmosphere?
Now the rage seems to be fracking,
Tho' it's been linked to the earth quaking;
It's hydraulic fracturing, breaking up rocks it,
While chemicals used are known to be toxic.
"But we still need natural gas and oil,"
Say those who care less what goes into the soil,
And into the water and air and food;
Less concerned with the greater good.
Surely there are other ways,
Like capturing the sun's many rays;
Geothermal, safer chemicals, even wind;
And we might even try much less wasting.
"What about nuclear power?" some say;
"That might be a better way."
But what if there are nuclear explosions,
And nuclear waste goes into our oceans,
And into our air and lakes and streams,
And soil and food and all living things?
The Earth may survive, the Earth we hold dear;
But as things are now, I have much fear.

The West Virginia Jacksons

———❦———

In the 1700s John and Elizabeth Cummins Jackson
Sailed on the same ship, immigrants from England.
Landed in Maryland and married in America;
Moved and made a family in (West) Virginia.
They crossed the Appalachians and were true pioneers;
They claimed vast lands in their new frontiers.
Elizabeth's husband John, and their sons Edward and George,
Went away to fight in the Revolutionary War.
It's otherwise known as the War for Independence;
Aptly named for more than one reason;
For the immigrants wanted to be freer than they felt in England.
It's been told that since Elizabeth helped defend Fort Jackson,
The new government recognized her service and gave her a pension.
She lived to be 101 and is buried in Harrison County, West Virginia.
In Clarksburg the Jacksons were community leaders,
And Edward and George were both colonels in the war.
George Jackson was a delegate to the Virginia Convention
To consider ratifying the new federal constitution.
In 1788 traveling Methodist Bishop Asbury
Passed through Clarksburg and stayed at George's ordinary.
Asbury had a prophetic, still relevant warning;
How the preaching of some "poisons them with error of doctrine";*
And warned about the "aristocracy of wealth" and lording over the poor;
Said "savage warfare teaches them to be cruel."
"And good Christians they cannot be, unless they are better taught";
Had more people paid attention some wars might have not been fought.

Edward said to be an ancestor of mine;
And it's said he also fought the Indian.
Indian attacks were part of life on the frontier;
And it was still dangerous to live in an exposed area;
And although Clarksburg had an academy and a courthouse,
In 1795 Indians killed a family that lived near;

Indian fighters stopped by and showed Jackson children fresh scalps.
I've read it took Clarksburg twenty years to build a church;
And for established religion the Jackson men didn't seem to think much.

George served three terms in the United States Congress,
And was on the House Committee on Indian Affairs.
He writes to his constituents in 1803 when he retires,
Warning of deficit spending, state religion, and Federalists.
George's son John was then elected to George's office,
And helped try to convict Aaron Burr of conspiracy.
(Now people are clamoring for Hamilton to see.)
John married Mary Payne, the sister of Dolly Madison,
The wife of the fourth president, James Madison.
The Jackson family had established national prominence.
(While many feel faceless and anonymous)

Edward Jackson had two wives and fifteen children;
He had moved from Clarksburg to Buckhannon.
His first wife, Mary, died and left George, David, Jonathan;
The boys ten, eight, six; Rachel four, Mary two, Rebecca an infant.
Jonathan the father of Thomas Jonathan
Jackson, later nicknamed Stonewall,
Whose father died when he was two and his mother when he was seven.
The day after their father died, Stonewall's sister Laura born;
Some said Stonewall was the greatest Civil War general of all;
Stonewall for the South, his sister for the Union;
And this brother and sister parted ways; more reason to mourn.
Stonewall died of complications after his own troops shot him;
When he lost his left arm, Lee said he'd lost his right arm.

Edward and Mary's David supposedly my ancestor;
He would become a fur trapper and trader and western explorer;
Around the time of the Louisiana purchase, he went roaming
To St Louis and beyond, to Jackson Hole, Wyoming;
Supposedly, Smith, Jackson and Sublette SJS wagons
Were the first wagons to cross the Rocky Mountains;
And they were among the first early Californians.
With other Oregon trailblazers and Lewis and Clark,
They helped map the country from the States to the Pacific.

According to family lore, my grand-father's mother Martha said
Her mother, Nancy, was proud of her cousin
Stonewall and her father David.
Martha said she remembered her mother talk of missing David, her father
While he was out West being a trapper and trader and explorer.
Told a story about Nancy, with no man at home,
Killed a deer and set a child's broken leg with the deer's leg bone.
Nancy had other mountain folks who fought in the Civil War,
Some for one side, some for the other;
But my grand-father's family were admirers of Lincoln;
And, like Stonewall's sister, I think I would have been for the Union.
Don't know why Stonewall didn't side with western Virginia,
Which became its own "Yankee" state when our nation would divide.
I read that Stonewall felt sorry for slaves when he was a child,
And thought they should learn to read so they could read the Bible.
Strange how some people think and their beliefs can reconcile.

David Jackson was away from home, of course
When he died in western Tennessee of typhus.
He was forty-nine and in a younger Paris.
Married to Juliet, the mother of four:
Edward, William, Nancy, Mary;
And with all his travels there might have been more.
He wrote detailed letters pertaining to his estate;
And like many in his day he owned a few slaves.
Paris had 800 people and twelve doctors of a sort;
David Jackson's doctor doubled as a clerk of court.
David was buried, like many other Jacksons,
In a cemetery in Lewis County, West Virginia.

So Nancy was the mother of my great-grandmother Martha;
As far as I know they never left North Carolina;
And Martha was the mother of my grand-father William;
And here's where it all gets very confusing.
Nancy and Martha are buried deep in some woods
At the foot of the mountains in McDowell County, North Carolina;
And David's daughter Nancy with Juliet buried
in Lewis County, West Virginia;
So David had two Nancys or my great-grandmother [without intent] lied;

But I think she told the story until the day she died.
I'm sure she believed it, but I can't find
Any evidence that David was ever in Caroline;
But we really don't know about Nancy Jackson Harris' mother;
We know that David traveled with another explorer;
There may be a connection with Moses "Black" Harris;
With swarthy skin, not black, it's said, but not from Paris;
Some said he was half Indian, and you better believe
Along the way there would be many a half breed.
Black Moses Harris was from Union County, South Caroline;
Maybe David's second daughter Nancy married Moses Harris' son.

Jackson is one of the most common twenty names in the USA;
Not that it matters who your folks are, I tend to say;
And although Andrew Jackson was born in Caroline;
I've found no connection and with that I'm fine.
For all I know Michael Jackson is my kin;
And he would likely be the one with the most talent;
He was born in Gary, Indiana;
And my ancestor Edward Jackson's daughter Eliza
Died eighty miles from Gary, in Mt Vernon, Indiana.

Some people love to learn their genealogy;
Their roots, their relatives they like to study;
Their ancestors and their place of birth;
But I sometimes question what it's really worth.
I think we need to appreciate the hardships endured
So those who come later could have it so good;
And I guess it's good to know if there are medical reasons,
And if there's a problem with your family's genes;
But what matters most is your current character;
Your here and now, not your ancient ancestor;
And how you are contributing to a better future.

*From main source Shadow on the Tetons: David E. Jackson and
the Claiming of the American West, by John C. Jackson, Mountain
Press Publishing Co, Missoula, Montana, 1993; quotes from p. 9.

Family Soldiers

From King's Mountain, Korea, Afghanistan, Iraq;
Before, between, within, beyond, near and far;
Our men kin have served in peace and in war;
And an aunt was even our county's first WAC.

To the war for independence
My grandma's great-great grandpa went;
Over the hills to King's Mountain
To fight the British; many years to win.
His tombstone says he was a hundred fourteen;
The oldest survivor known around here.
Maybe William Davis the oldest of all men
To serve in any war anywhere.

Grandma's grandpa at Gettysburg was killed;
But William's daughter Peggy's sons, at Gettysburg, lived;
Came back home, lived some fifty years,
With stories and more, of valor and fears.
They say that Peggy walked to Richmond,
Where her youngest son was in Army prison;
Many miles across the mountain land
To prove him too young, with Bible in hand.
The "three Wise men," as they were known;
Peggy (Margaret) Wise's Tom and Newton and John;
They fought for the South, to my chagrin;
Came back home and taught some Latin.

And then there was great-grandma's cousin;
General Stonewall Jackson, no less;
Lee's "right arm," lost his left arm, then his life;
His sister for the North; me too, I guess.

As for World War I or others not recalled

I know of no ties with my family at all.
My daddy too young for WWI, too old for II,
And after he joined he went AWOL.

But many served in World War II;
Most in Europe, the Pacific, too;
On the ground, in the air, on the water;
One in Hawaii, glad it wasn't Okinawa.
My uncle and cousins, three were brothers;
I can't help but think of all of the mothers;
My grand-parents' child and four grandsons;
All at war while the birth of a son of one
Who reached Normandy soon after D-Day;
Was wounded in more than one fray;
Led a platoon, where all others died;
While he alone, with guilt, survived;
A month before his first child arrived.
Awoke on a truck, with dead all around;
Thrown on the truck or left on the ground;
Nephews in Europe, new baby at home;
Wonder what they were doing in Rome?

While Jews were robbed and chased and caught;
Why is it that most churches said and did naught?
While Nazis killed, imprisoned, gassed,
Many listened to Hitler, whose time didn't last.
And what about Italy and Japan?
What were they thinking, joining in?
With awful Hitler, an evil man,
Promising to make things great again.
Russia our ally, imagine that;
They lost many millions; God it was bad;
Bombs over London, Tokyo, and Berlin;
If God was watching, why wasn't He helping?

Back at home, they were doing their part;
Sacrifice, rationing, women at work;
Rosie the Riveter, many others,
Like the Women's Auxiliary Corps.

Glenn a pilot before he could drive;
Over Yugoslavia his plane on fire;
Bailed with brothers to the ground,
Missing in action, but came home sound.
Lee in Europe for three long years;
Learned so much German
He made it a teaching career.
The Pacific, too, and he's still here!
And there was Roy, the roughest boy;
A brave Marine, the best uniform;
World War II, later Vietnam;
Korea between, a tough Marine.

Hitler a suicide; the Jews they were freed;
But millions dead, starvation and need.
What were they thinking those Japanese?
Two nukes dropped down to bring them to their knees.

Russia, too, developed nuclear,
And decided to keep the satellite states.
China then, too, became Communist;
And then we had a new Cold War.

Korea was bad; there's no good war;
Danny McGee and Cousin Clyde went there;
Danny much too young, still a teen;
They wouldn't say what they had seen.
Marine cousin Jim before Guantanamo
On Orange Bowl team with Duke football;
But this Cold War it was no game;
The Cuban missile crisis scary as they came.
Brother Joe got out during Vietnam;
After Alaska, Formosa/Taiwan, Germany, missile silos;
But when Vietnam came it was time to go.

The draft at eighteen of many young men
Who couldn't vote until age twenty-one;
Some dodgers and deferments offered to some;
Or medical reasons; I can't really blame them.

(But I find it a disgrace and a national shame
That we have a POTUS without a clue;
Who bragged fighting STDs was his Vietnam,
Who insulted Sen McCain for being a POW,
After all the suffering so many went through.)

Cousins Stan and Ron left UNC;
To a big war in Vietnam from a big university.
Brothers and their parents' only sons;
The Tet Offensive; sons behind their guns.
Their parents prayed, I would believe;
With GI Bill, they finished UNC;
High school heroes, basketball stars;
It takes all types to fight our wars.
Stan would be nominated for a Pulitzer;
Ron would become a college official.
Now Cousin Stan has cancer of the lung;
Can't help but wonder about Agent Orange.

My son wished to go to Desert Storm;
Still in high school, with a pacifist mom.
Soon as he could, he decided to join;
He's still a soldier; still in the Army.
A mountain boy from early on,
Killed his first bear when he was eleven;
An Army Ranger known for daring,
Teaching other Rangers mountaineering.
A young US soldier who trained in Russia;
Later four plus years in Afghanistan, special operations;
Alaska, Yemen, Oman, Kyrgystan, Africa time and again
Jade Helm, no telling where else, other -stans.

He asked me why I didn't serve
During Vietnam. Did I have the nerve?
As a girl I had the right
To not be drafted and called to fight.
Do I feel guilty? Yes and no;
For women haven't had to go
To war and fight and hurt and die;

For that I'm glad; I cannot lie.
Yet many go now and do their service;
Pilots, fighters, Rangers, nurses.
Now gay and straight can ask and tell;
The jury's still out about transgenders;
Too many think LGBTs should go to Hell;
I say be themselves; just be good soldiers.

Some soldiers served in the Guard or Reserves;
They're sometimes called "week-end warriors."
Brother Ed got called from reserve to active duty
To train troops for Iraq at Fort Jackson (as in Andrew).
After serving in Germany before the Berlin Wall came down;
And in South Korea in the Army near the demilitarized zone;
Soon Ed's older son Matthew went to war in Iraq;
With wife, four children, other family at home;
A Guardsman worker on planes; he made it back;
Came home to them by Christmas time.
Ed's younger son Chad has joined, too;
Willing to serve, to do his Army duty;
Now he may go to Iraq after Djibouti.

Other kith and kin in wars through the years;
Fighting for us through all their fears;
Too few rich and too many poor
Go away to fight in war.
They serve us all, our way of life;
Let's try to make it worth their strife.
Better to avoid war, I say;
Reminded it's not so simple, this anniversary of D-Day.

D-Day Anniversary

More than seventy years,
But we think of their fears;
Those on the shore, in air, those in water;
Many were destined to face sure slaughter.
American airmen, sailors, soldiers;
The Brits, Canadians, many others;
From many countries, they became brothers
In this fight for what is right.
An epic day in modern times
Far away in Normandy;
While I'm at home making rhymes;
The least I can do to remember D-Day.
Who would dream
We would later befriend
Our fearsome foes?
No one knows what the future holds.

If You Can't Defend Your Cousin

"If you can't defend your cousin
How can you defend your country?"
These were words a mother asked her teenage son.
Since he wished to be soldier,
Like many family before him,
She was proud but said we need you first at home.
"There is trouble with your cousin
And the man that she's been seeing;
She's not free because he beats her, that I know;
So please help your cousin before you go."

"You see, about 50,000 of our men died in Vietnam;
And those same years in our country
About 50,000 US men killed their woman;
And if your cousin's not free her world's not free;
So take care of your cousin, please, before your country."
So the young man helped his cousin,
And he learned a lifelong lesson;
Then he went to serve his country, you and me.

Hunter Soldier

He gained local fame when his picture
Appeared in the county's newspaper;
His first bear kill when he was eleven;
He'd been hunting since he was seven.
In the newspaper picture his chest was bare;
His arm around the neck of the dead black bear;
His shirt off although it was fall;
Made him look like the toughest kid of all.
It was the first day of bear hunting season;
His mother was worried and for good reason.
She wouldn't ever buy him a toy gun,
But when he was seven she lost custody of her son.
The bear kill in North Carolina on Mt Mitchell,
The highest mountain east of the Mississippi.
"He kilt one!" said the little hunter's grandmother,
When she answered the phone that night and it was his mother.
When his mother asked, "One what?" She said, "He kilt a bar!"
At a church homecoming a few months later
His mother talked with another hunter;
He was on Mt Mitchell the day of the kill,
And the man had a little story to tell.
Her son called the hunter on his walkie talkie;
(Do hunters still use such technology?)
Said he saw a bear, told him his location.
(This was before we became a cellphone nation.)
The man heard the bear growl; then there was nothing.
The man rushed to the boy, fearing what he would find;
Rushing over rocks and steep dangerous terrain;
When he got to the boy he had killed the bear with his gun;
Hunters are different in the ways they have fun.

A hunter may eat the kill, like a bear or deer steak;
This boy hunter took another kill for his granny to cook;

Then before karate class he got a strange look;
When asked what he was eating, replied, "Rattlesnake."
Got his black belt in karate before his license to drive;
It's a miracle this hunter soldier is still alive.
When he was nine his appendix would rupture;
The doctor who delivered him assisted in the surgery.
When his mother got to him later that night,
The doctor only added to her fright;
Told her, "He's still not out of the woods";
But this little hunter was tough in the woods.
I don't know whether prayers were a factor,
But within a week, to her shock, he was driving a tractor.
Long before he was old enough to get a driver's license,
He was driving a tractor on the farm and far beyond;
His mother has had little control but lots of concern,
From when he was very young and all years since.
By age sixteen the boy owned twelve guns;
Or was it by age twelve he owned sixteen guns?
Sold an automatic rifle to a Baptist preacher;
At seventeen; makes no sense to me; go figure.
His mother said, "There's another way to shoot an animal";
And for Christmas one year she bought him a camera.
He helped kill a second but not a third bear;
His interests would take him elsewhere by far.

In high school not aiming for college,
But best in his class on a test in biology;
Not interested in Spanish, he told the teacher,
"All I need to know is tequila and senorita."
Studying the globe he'd take to his desk;
Showing no interest on some tests.
When asked to write about an ideal vacation,
It wasn't about an expected location.
He wanted to go see Vietnam,
And he wanted to fight in Desert Storm.
At age eighteen he joined the Army;
Delayed a few weeks because of a knee;
Said he'd be in the military
If he had to become a mercenary.

Ft Benning, Ft Bragg, Ranger school, Alaska;
Among the first US troops to train in Russia.
No surprise to his family or fellow hunter,
He became an Army Ranger mountaineering instructor.
Then green beret's special ops service would take him far;
Dinner in London with British troops and the Queen's guard.
Meetings at the Pentagon, with more respect
Than some who haven't worn a bullet-proof vest.
Don't know how much he's used the Arabic he learns;
Goes to Germany, Africa, the UAE, Kyrgystan;
Four total years in Afghanistan, fighting against the Taliban;
And working to win hearts and minds;
The way to win a war of another kind.
Sent him food and supplies for an Afghan clinic;
Something aid workers don't find unique.
Sent medical books, not in Dari or Farsi;
Anatomy and physiology, pediatrics, cardiology;
A good variety of others for treatment and diagnosis;
The doctor needed for the clinic and could read English.
A smart green beret, special operations;
No telling what and where other stations;
Still in one piece with two good knees;
Through gunfire, IEDs, jumps from planes;
And heavy hikes over rough terrains;
Still strong, still tough, no signs of PTSD.
With so much tragedy, we've still been lucky.

Just one of many hunter soldiers;
Shooting and shot at and many adventures;
Shooting people and also pictures;
Dealing with shady and decent peoples;
Shots of elephants, lions, other dangerous creatures;
But doubt many can say they killed a bear
When only eleven; and for his senior year
His mother made payments on him a new Jeep
That for several years he would keep;
With a sign on the windshield that said, "No Fear."
But one of the best stories I think you'll read here
Is about when he was a young soldier,

108

And his grandfather was dying of cancer.
He went to the hospital where his grandpaw's doctor was working,
The same hospital where that doctor, a Vietnam vet, delivered him;
(The same doctor who sewed up his hand when he was a teen,
On his way with his uncle to shoot at a musket competition;
Around the time he took pride that his jeans could stand alone,
Like they might have back in the days of Daniel Boone.)
Took all his grandpaw's many medicines and started asking,
"What should Grandpaw take and when should he take them?"
Great Dr George Ellis suggested he take military leave;
(Dr Ellis had been a young U.S. Army doctor in Vietnam)
He did and got to spend time with his grandpaw and help him;
I hope being there with family helped lessen his grief.
He's since had several brothers-in-arms and friends
Become casualties; some PTSD, some life and death wounds.
He's gone to be with family during several funerals;
Like the time he had to leave a family picnic,
When he got a call a buddy was killed in Afghanistan or Iraq.
He's given eulogies when I don't see how he hasn't cried;
Been with family when a child was told his daddy has died.
He doesn't talk of fear, but it has to be there.
He won't tell me much; I have to pry;
I'll be proud of him until the day I die.

JFK and Other Deaths

Countless others have considered a conspiracy
About the death of President John F Kennedy
In Dallas, Texas on November 22, 1963.
There are still too many questions about the death of JFK
For us to consider it another way;
And I'm almost ashamed to say I always suspected LBJ.
Maybe just my imagination, my mind's invention,
But there's something to be said for women's intuition.
I heard Bobby and Jack would ridicule Lyndon,
Which might have given him intention;
And he would no longer be second.
And I wouldn't doubt the role of Nixon;
And here are some other reasons for suspicion:

Kennedy in August '63 had paid the speech attention
Of Rev Dr Martin Luther King Jr and the civil rights movement;
And was planning to take action toward King's dream
When conservatives would call King a Communist;
Trying to discredit him when there was no good evidence.
Also, Kennedy might have stopped the war in Vietnam,
And Johnson could make a fortune with Halliburton.
Texan Johnson one of many a crony;
Who knows what all they've done for money?
And it's reported Johnson told his mistress;
Suggested to her he did it, to her he'd near confess.
I'm not a fan of Roger Stone, who wrote a book blaming LBJ;
And I liked LBJ's fight for civil rights, healthcare and the rest,
But my suspicions of him still won't go away.

There was a major investigation by the Warren Commission,
Which concluded Lee Harvey Oswald acted alone;
But on the Commission was a Congressman;
Gerald Ford, who in the report changed a sentence,
Giving conspiracy theorists' more suspicion.

Surprisingly (or not) some even blame the CIA;
For several reasons they were upset with JFK.
They blamed him for the failure of the Bay of Pigs invasion;
And maybe because he wanted a Castro-Cuba relation.
Maybe he didn't work with them like Eisenhower;
Maybe their relationship had gone too sour.
Were Frank Sturgis and E Howard Hunt really there?
Or Ed Lansdale or Charles Harrelson, as some say;
Some even suggest James Earl Ray!
Former CIA Director Allen Dulles was on the Warren Commission;
And the future CIA Director was said that fateful day to be in Dallas;
Appointed by Ford when he was president, he was George HW Bush.
His photo at the school book depository (or Ed
Lansdale's in Dallas) may not be real;
But why a note to J Edgar Hoover, and did Bush really giggle
When speaking of Kennedy's death at Gerald Ford's funeral?

This matter might be more easily laid to rest
If there weren't so many possibly related deaths.
It even goes back to gorgeous Marilyn Monroe
Who supposedly died of an overdose the year before.
She and President Kennedy apparently had an affair,
Which could obviously affect his presidency's future.
Kennedy could get away with such things,
And supposedly with many women had flings;
But it's said Marilyn was going to tell the world;
Yes, she was depressed, had been a messed-up girl;
Some say she didn't overdose, that she was killed;
And that Robert Kennedy, it's even been told;
Who was Attorney General, maybe played a role.
Perhaps President Kennedy's most enduring other woman,
In addition to beautiful Jacqueline, his wife,
Was lovely Mary Meyer who lost her life.
She was murdered on a path in Georgetown in October '64
Some said the KGB had it in for Kennedy and her;
It happens that her ex-husband was a CIA officer.
I've even read that JFK had an affair
With a female Russian agent during the Cold War.

Adding to the mystery of the death of John Kennedy
Was that the suspect had connections to Russia and Cuba.
Kennedy's alleged killer Oswald was killed two days later
By a Dallas night club owner named Jack Ruby,
Who supposedly had connections to the mafia.
But did Oswald have connections to the CIA?
How could Ruby know just where Oswald would be
When Oswald was in Dallas police custody?
It seems the way Ruby shot him was too easy,
As he was being escorted with police all around;
And Jack Ruby's true motive was really not found.
Oswald shouted he was a patsy, if that means anything;
And to this day we don't know what Oswald sang.
Oswald and his Russian wife had moved to Dallas
Not long after he met her in Russia.
In Dallas they made an unlikely acquaintance,
A rich man by the name of George de Mohrenschildt,
From Russia but supposedly with the CIA.
And why did Oswald go to Mexico City to the US Embassy?
Was he being set up? It wasn't for fun;
And did de Mohrenschildt get Oswald the job where he fired the gun?

Supposedly John F Kennedy's rich father Joe
Made a deal with the devil, Sam Giancana, others also;
Said if they got his son votes in Cook County, Chicago;
That if John got elected, he'd get rid of Fidel Castro;
Which meant the mafia could get back in Havana
And re-open places like the Tropicana and Copacabana;
But when JFK failed to fulfill his father's deal,
Maybe the mob killed John F Kennedy for real.

Many more mysterious deaths--suicides, murders, crashes;
More than a hundred have met a questionable fate.
Everyone dies, but most not these ways;
Seems some must be connected, can't be all coincidence.
We all heard about officer JD Tippett,
Allegedly shot by Oswald soon after he shot the president.
Jack Zangetty, a motel manager in Oklahoma,
Reportedly told some friends he had overheard a conversation;

112

And that three men, not Oswald, had done the assassination;
And that Ruby would kill Oswald the very next day.
Jack Zangetty was found shot two weeks later,
Floating dead in a lake after he went away.
A phone operator in LA reported that Karyn Kupcinet
Was screaming into a phone that Kennedy was going to be shot.
Karyn was found murdered in her home two days after the event.
When a suspicious reporter named Bill Hunter
Was shot with a policeman's revolver
In the Dallas police station in April '64 in the heart,
The policeman claimed it was an accident.
Tom Howard was Ruby's chief attorney and spokesman for awhile;
Howard knew Hunter and a few months later Howard died.
Howard was dropped off by who knows at a Dallas hospital;
Doctor said a heart attack at age 48 but no autopsy.

Lisa Howard was ABC's first female news anchor;
She went to Cuba in '63 and interviewed Castro;
A liaison for Kennedy, improving US-Cuba relations was a role;
ABC fired her for being too political in the fall of '64.
In December she hosted for Che Guevara a cocktail party
When he came and spoke at the United Nations in New York City.
Could Che have been the father when in June '65
she had a miscarriage and was morose?
On July 4th on vacation in the Hamptons,
she supposedly died of a barbiturate overdose.
Dorothy Kilgallen was another nationally well-known reporter;
The only one to get a one-to-one interview with Jack Ruby.
It was said she died of an overdose in November '65,
In good spirits after appearing earlier that night on a TV show live.
And there was the war correspondent Marguerite Higgins;
Covered World War II, Korea, and Vietnam.
Seems she accused the CIA of the '63 killings
Of Premier Ngo and his brother Nhu Diem;
And herself died January '66 in a landmine explosion.

Earlene Roberts ran the rooming house where Oswald lived in Dallas.
Seems after he shot Kennedy he came home and got another gun;
Maybe used it to kill Tippett, but that wasn't all;

She suggested two police pulled up and honked a signal
To Oswald when she testified in Dallas in '64 in April;
After that police harassed her and she died in the same hospital
Where Kennedy was taken; she in January '66, a heart attack.
Warren Reynolds ran a used car lot in Dallas;
He heard Tippett get shot and gave chase.
He seemed unsure whether the shooter was Oswald.
Supposedly, two days after talking to the FBI he was shot in the head;
Alone, at night, at the car lot, nothing stolen, but survived.
He was supposedly harassed and threatened until he ID'd Oswald.
Nancy Jane Mooney, alias, Betty McDonald,
Gave an alibi for Darrell Wayne Garner,
Who had bragged that he shot Warren Reynolds.
After she was arrested for disturbing the peace,
According to the Dallas police report,
She hanged herself February '64 with her toreador pants
She wore to work at Jack Ruby's Carousel Club.
Rose Cherami might not have been the most credible;
She supposedly did drugs, worked at Ruby's
Club, warned of Kennedy's death;
And was killed by a hit and run September '65 in Texas.
Delilah Walle was working on a book about what she knew;
She died when her new husband shot her; she had also worked for Ruby.
Also odd is what happened to Hank Killam;
Obsessed with JFKs death and why Oswald killed him.
His wife Wanda had worked for Jack Ruby, it's said;
Killam supposedly an acquaintance and maybe cohort of Oswald.
He moved from Dallas to Florida, and it appears he was paranoid.
Supposedly Federal agents followed him, and whether true or not,
After a phone call on St Patrick's Day in '64 he went out on the street.
He was found on a sidewalk and bled to death with his jugular vein cut.
Domingo Benavides witnessed the murder of JD Tippett,
But he wasn't sure it was Oswald who did it.
His look-alike brother Eddy shot fatally in February '64;
Their father shot but survived in Dallas two weeks later.
Gary Underhill, a former CIA agent, an apparent suicide, shot in May '64;
About the death of Kennedy, he claimed he knew more.
William Whaley was the cabbie who, after the Kennedy shooting,
Drove Oswald near his home; did Oswald talk while he was riding?

Whaley ID'd Oswald in a line-up;
died December '65 in a head-on collision;
The first Dallas cab driver to die in nearly
thirty years on duty in such a crash.
Lee Bowers was a witness to JFK's assassination;
He testified of suspicious activity to the Warren Commission;
Said a motorcycle policeman left the motorcade after a commotion;
Went toward two mysterious men who maybe fired from the grassy knoll;
In August '66 Bowers' brand new car hit a bridge abutment;
Age 41, he died in a Dallas hospital and was cremated.
His widow supposedly said, "They told him not to talk."
William Waters supposedly called the FBI to report
He heard Oswald and Killam talking about the assassination;
Supposedly the FBI told him to keep his mouth shut;
He was arrested and in jail for months in Memphis;
And police said he died in May '67 of a drug overdose.
Albert Guy Bogard, a Lincoln Mercury salesman,
Said he showed a car to Oswald, told the Commission;
Soon after he was badly beaten and later found dead;
Ruled a suicide, with a hose in his car attached to the exhaust.

Jack Ruby apparently had mobster connections;
And likely had illegal dealings such as prostitution;
And some people say he was involved in gun running.
After Castro took over, Ruby in '59 went to Cuba,
Perhaps with his intentions, to no avail;
No reason to think he met with Fidel.
Maybe Oswald was a failed Russian agent;
Any way one views him leads to no satisfaction;
Which perhaps still leads many to question
If with JFK's death there's a Soviet or Cuba connection.
After all, the Cuban Missile Crisis was just a little more than a year before,
When the world was on edge with fear of a nuclear war;
But the failed Bay of Pigs invasion the year before that as well
Might have had more to do with why Kennedy would die.
There's still no known connection with Nikita or Fidel;
That Khrushchev or Castro caused it, but of course people lie.

And how could I not mention the death of Che Guevara?

Whether you think him a revolutionary hero or a pariah,
His death hardly a cover-up by the CIA,
Who helped find him and kill him in October '67 in Bolivia.

As if it's not dreary and weird enough, it only gets weirder;
There's even speculation about experimental cancer.
No question that Jack Ruby should go to prison;
He shot Oswald in front of millions;
We watched it live on TV after Thanksgiving.
Ruby got sick in prison and went to Parkland Hospital;
He had a pulmonary embolism and lung cancer; it had spread;
In a few weeks in January '67 Jack Ruby was dead.
He was framed to kill Oswald some say he said;
Others say he denied a conspiracy on his death bed.
David Ferrie of New Orleans died the next month.
All of this is surely not just coincidence.

Ferrie was a rabid anti-Communist who supposedly had said
After the failed Bay of Pigs that Kennedy should be dead.
He had been a pilot in the Civil Air Patrol
The same time Oswald served there but denied any role.
According to the Church Committee hearings,
Six credible witnesses said they saw Ferrie in New Orleans
With Lee Harvey Oswald in September '63.
Eladio Cerefine de Valle was associated with Ferrie;
Supposedly he was ID'ing Oswald and others
for New Orleans DA Jim Garrison;
And died the same day as Ferrie, shot and his skull split open.
After Ferrie died, New Orleans DA Jim Garrison believed
That since Ferrie left two suicide notes he didn't die a natural death.
But Ferrie's death somehow said caused by a natural brain bleed.
So strange how so many had their last breath.
The next month Garrison arrested Clay Shaw for JFK death conspiracy,
Trying hard to unravel all the mystery.
It seems David Ferrie, along with Clay Shaw and Guy Banister,
Worked out of a New Orleans office of CIA operations on Latin America.
Those three musketeers were known as right-wing extremists,
Who then, as now, were likely racists and bigots.
In the John Birch Society? A private detective? A former FBI agent?

116

An Assistant Superintendent of the New Orleans Police Department?
Guy Banister had died of a heart attack in June '64;
Or was it, as some claimed they saw, from a bullet hole?
Banister's business partner Hugh Ward within ten days died,
In a plane crash perhaps with others with CIA ties.
Some think David Ferrie, Clay Shaw, and Guy Banister were three men
Who were part of a conspiracy to set up Oswald as a patsy back then;
That they hated Kennedy over peace efforts and civil rights,
And would conspire against Kennedy to fight their fights.

But what about cancer? Here's the weirdest part:
The month after Guy Banister died of a bullet hole in his heart,
One of David Ferrie's friends was found murdered.
She was Dr Mary Sherman, a New Orleans cancer researcher,
Who was supposedly doing a cancer experiment with David Ferrie.
So some really think David Ferrie somehow gave cancer to Jack Ruby
And perhaps to Paul Dyer, said to be the first New
Orleans policeman to question Ferrie.
Dyer got sick and died of cancer in a month
soon after he interviewed Ferrie.
Dr Nicholas Chetta was the New Orleans
coroner who had served since 1950;
And when David Ferrie supposedly died of a brain hemorrhage,
And against Clay Shaw he was the key witness,
Dr Chetta died in May '69 of an apparent heart attack at age fifty.
The only person ever charged in JFK's death was Clay Shaw alone;
A New Orleans jury quickly acquitted him, embarrassing Jim Garrison.
You can see some of this in the JFK movie by Oliver Stone.
Shaw, too, died of lung cancer in August '74, a heavy smoker, age 61.

John Crawford, a Jack Ruby friend, died in a
plane crash in Texas in April '69;
His neighbor drove Oswald to work the day of the Kennedy killing.
Then there's the death of Cliff Carter, an LBJ aide,
Who was riding in Dallas in the JFK motorcade.
Carter died in Washington DC mysteriously
of pneumonia in September '71;
Supposedly when for some reason he couldn't get penicillin.
Hale Boggs was Democrat Congressional Whip from New Orleans,

117

And he served with Ford and others on the Warren Commission.
There are different accounts of whether he agreed to the conclusions,
When many hoped the investigation would be over;
But in April '71 he strongly attacked the whole FBI and J Edgar Hoover.
Minority leader Ford and President Nixon were
dismayed, and the FBI of course;
In October '72, in a twin-engine plane in Alaska, he was lost in a crash.
Roger Dean Craig witnessed the JFK assassination as a Dallas policeman,
But his story was different from the rest of them;
The police supposedly threatened and harassed
him, tho' in '61 he was named their best;
His wife left him and he died in May '75 when he shot himself in the chest.

Strangely, in 1977 there is a letter
From one George to another; one is deader;
From de Mohrenschildt to Bush, head of the CIA;
He sounds paranoid and desperate, not saying why,
But he's afraid he's going to die;
Not long afterward he was an apparent suicide.
Sure, there seem to be copious cover-ups, as many agree;
Even with former Fox Bill O'Reilly's book Killing Kennedy;
For some reason O'Reilly doesn't mention that de Mohrenschildt
Could have been involved in Kennedy getting killed.
Bill, how about telling us all the rest you know?
And a couple of years ago I watched a TV show
About ballistics evidence, trajectories, gun testing,
Related to Kennedy's assassination.
(Didn't trust the findings when I saw it got Koch funding.)

Another documentary with different expert opinion
Takes away trust in the Warren Commission and adds confusion.
Ballistics expert Howard Donahue had another theory,
Which seemed to make some sense to me.
Supposedly, several witnesses saw Secret Service Agent George Hickey
Stand up in a motorcade car with an AR-15 that possibly also shot Kennedy.
Nearby witnesses reported smelling gunpowder;
There's a book about this titled Mortal Error;
Saying Oswald hit Kennedy twice, then Hickey accidentally once;
I would think such an event more than coincidence.

118

The documentary about this suggests a Secret Service cover-up
To protect one of their possibly innocent own and keep it hush-hush.
Or could it have been something more nefarious?

I didn't trust Johnson and doubt anyone trusts Nixon;
They were the two with the most to gain;
And did Nixon know something that really
caused Johnson to not run again?
Johnson faced unprecedented protests over the draft and Vietnam War,
But he had gotten many more votes than
Goldwater in '64 so was there more?
When Robert Kennedy announced he was going to run,
Like his brother, he seemed much better than Nixon.
Many of us felt new reason to realistically wish
For what Robert Kennedy could accomplish.
Many were protesting and police and others attacking them,
And many of our soldiers and others were getting killed in Vietnam.
Four young black girls had been killed by a bomb in church
A few weeks before JFK's death; how can people endure so much?
Great Martin Luther King Jr was killed in April 1968,
And two months later Robert Kennedy would meet his fate;
Had Sirhan Sirhan not shot him, he would likely have been President,
But Nixon became the next White House resident.

Something else that raises my suspicion
Is the shooting of George Wallace when he was running against Nixon.
Wallace was shot (not killed) campaigning in May of '72;
Had Wallace not dropped out of the race when
shot, Nixon had the most to lose.
By the way, Lyndon Johnson died two days
after Nixon's second inauguration.
Then the Watergate conspiracy scandal, Ford's
pardon, and Nixon's resignation.
And some suspects in Watergate some said were at Kennedy's assassination.

After Nixon resigned, the Church Committee formed by Congress
To investigate national intelligence and some of these deaths.
Seems they concluded JFK's death probably a
conspiracy but Oswald the shooter;

And MLK's death a small conspiracy but James Earl Ray the shooter;
(Don't think they implicated the CIA or FBI or J Edgar Hoover);
Concluded the report of the Warren Commission was lacking;
So, we don't really know who conspirators were backing.
We're left with questions of who we can trust;
Troubling; for a country to be good trust is a must.

I've even read Robert Kennedy's convicted killer, it is theorized;
Sirhan Sirhan, still in prison, the CIA might have hypnotized.
Wish we could trust all we read and hear;
So much we still don't know but it seems rather clear;
When you get too close to truth there may be much to fear.

Now for an update: Something I heard on TV last night;
I think on National Geographic Channel, trying to shed more light.
Some Kennedy death government files are now declassified.
(The Warren Commission may have erred, omitted, and/or lied.)
Oswald had moved from New Orleans to Dallas only a few weeks before;
And, oddly, got a job on the Kennedy parade route at the book depository;
And in New Orleans (where Jack Ruby had connections) he worked not far
From a couple of places with suspected CIA ties; quite bizarre.

To the best of my knowledge all this poem is true;
But to be honest I'm not at all sure.
We hear more and more about fake news and disinformation,
(Even from big liars themselves leading our nation)
But we must have truth to have a better nation.

*Sources were largely Wikipedia and article "Disappearing Witnesses" by Penn Jones Jr, The Rebel magazine, January 1984 (http://www.maebrussell. com/Disappearing%20Witnesses..., obtained 5/22/2013)

Che Guevara

Che was handsome but so much more;
His main intent to help the poor;
So what if I'm driven in part by pulchritude,
When what should count is for right, for rectitude.

Like so many revolutionaries
Throughout many centuries;
Ideologies like communism their inventions;
The road to Hell paved with good intentions.

Che not the first doctor to give up medicine;
To find another calling in a revolution;
He went from saving lives and treating lepers
To killing enemies and treating fellow soldiers.

Ernesto (later Che) in Guatemala in 1954;
Cold War times; who would rule the world?
Some said the answer is capitalism;
Others said the answer is communism.
Rich United Fruit in Guatemala and the USA
Paid banana workers a few cents a day;
President Arbenz said to give the workers land;
President Eisenhower said to get rid of Arbenz.
John Foster Dulles was Secretary of State;
He had served on the board of United Fruit;
And what happened next explains Che's hate;
Allen Dulles of the CIA said, "We'll back a coup."
The United States, with our CIA
Helped massacre supporters of good President Arbenz
Who admired our FDR and much about the USA;
The coup among the worst of US sins.
Ernesto (later Che) fled to the Argentina embassy;
Then the Argentine went to Mexico City.

In Guatemala after Arbenz fled,
Many years of civil war and much bloodshed.

In Mexico City Ernesto met committed Cubans;
Castro and others planning revolution;
Dedicated and determined for their country;
His new comrades called him Che;
(Born Ernesto Guevara de la Serna in Argentina)
Fidel had already tried to oust Cuba's Batista;
Had led an attack on an army barracks in Cuba;
Arrested, imprisoned, then Batista released him;
Big mistake by Batista; what was he thinking?
In Mexico City the Cubans arrested;
About thirty of them for immigration;
And Che, too, for the same reason,
Spent nearly two summer months in a Mexican prison.

Then, around the time of our Thanksgiving,
Eighty-two set sail on the Caribbean;
Weeks after Ike won his second election;
In '56, onward to Cuba for their revolution.
Not over the river and through the woods
To Grandmother's house they'd go;
But on an old too small yacht called Granma.
Over the sea and into the woods to face their foe.
A ferocious foe, the rebels lean;
Batista's troops killed all but fifteen;
Fidel, Raul, Che, a dozen others;
Armed and dangerous, a band of brothers.
Swarms of mosquitoes, little food;
Gunfire and danger, Che had a wound;
Hunger, thirst, weak and worn;
Drinking swamp water, tough and strong.

The Cubans, the Castros, had help at home;
There had been several years of planning
Among Cuban men and also women,
Wanting better for Cuba than the Batista regime.

Aleida (Che's wife), Celia close to Fidel, Haydee,
Hilda (Che's first wife, from Peru)
Lidia, Melba, Natalia, Vilma (went to MIT, married to Raul);
Formed alliances and assemblies, handed out pamphlets;
Wives, lovers, others, strategy, support, some skillful combatants.

Few grieved more than Haydee Santamaria;
She was thrown in jail after Moncada;
So was her fiance Boris and her brother Abel;
They were tortured and killed to get them to tell.

From Moncado barracks and Guatemala;
La Plata, Sierra Maestra, Santa Clara to Havana;
After Che joined them he had a moment;
And in six months promoted to Comandante.
It doesn't seem quite right
For a doctor to war and fight;
But when Che had to make a decision,
He decided to pick up the weapon.

The rebels were able to win hearts and minds,
And many Cubans hated Batista's crimes.
They found that many Cubans would care
Enough to help them fight their guerrilla warfare.
In early 1959 with the rebels on their way
Batista fled Cuba on New Year's Day
Two days later into Havana rode Che;
Five days later Fidel made his way.

Over two years the rebels fought a larger army,
And Che wrote a book about guerrilla insurgency.
An intellectual, a multi-faceted man,
Che became a prominent Argentine Cuban.
Batista supporters who faced capture,
Were shot without trial; Che played a part.
It seems he didn't go along with torture;
I want to think he had more heart.

Back in the US the rebels were heroes;
That's before some rebels and everyone knows;
Because Fidel Castro was coy and cunning;
He had even used American gun running.
Fidel even toured the USA;
Che toured Europe, Africa, Asia;
Fidel met with Vice President Nixon,
But not with President Ike in 1959.

The story goes Castro needed an economist;
Che spoke up when he thought he heard "a communist";
Che then got a surprising rank;
He became the president of Cuba's National Bank.
Che was also the head of Cuba's agrarian reforms,
Which meant the government was taking over farms;
Not just sugar cane for Pepsi, but oil refineries too;
Nationalizing US companies not a smart thing to do.
The Cubans started courting the Soviet Union, China also;
In the United States there is much woe;
Cuba has turned to their Cold War foe;
The US imposes a partial, later a total embargo.
Seems Raul had visited Russia years ago;
And Che now visits the communist bloc;
The Russians, East Germans, Chinese, North Korea, Czechoslovaks
Many Cubans, some rebels, leave Cuba in shock.

President Kennedy elected in 1960;
Shortly thereafter Ike closes the Cuban embassies.
Che becomes Cuban Minister of Industry;
The CIA starts plotting with Cuban emigrants.
Kennedy promised publicly no US attack;
But many who fled Cuba want to take their nation back.
A day or two later the April '61 Bay of Pigs invasion;
In three days, a hundred plus dead, a thousand plus in Cuban prison.
Kennedy dismayed, five US bombers shot down;
Minister of Armed Forces Raul doesn't fool around.
Fidel as Prime Minister virtually dictates;
Sends Che to speak at OAS conference of Latin American States.

Then in 1962, the memorable month of October;
The Cuban Missile crisis came close to nuclear war.
Don't think Che ever forgot Guatemala,
And let nukes from Russia be ninety miles from Florida.
Khrushchev backed down, now Kennedy a hero;
Guess some Russians said Khrushchev should go.
It seems Che didn't care if the Soviets killed us;
Would sacrifice Cuba; if true, deranged, I guess;
Cooler minds prevailed; the Soviets removed the missiles.
All but nine Bay of Pig prisoners released around Christmas;
And Cuba would get an expensive gift;
Fifty million dollars in medical supplies; they were pleased.
In 1986 the last prisoner released.

November 22, 1963 Kennedy shot by an assassin,
Supposedly with ties to the Soviet Union.
And, of course many people said a Castro conspiracy;
It seems that wasn't true, and it's still a mystery.

Che obsessed and with brilliance and eloquence;
In 1964 he spoke at the United Nations.
He traveled through Africa, to broader horizons;
Left his work in Cuba to widen revolution.
Revolution in his blood, more than his kin;
His wife seemed to accept it, as did his children.
He led other Cubans to a Congo expedition
To assist a failed attempt unlike his Cuban revolution.
Che's goal to spread communism;
Wrongly called for "two, three, many Vietnams"
At a big Africa, Asia, Latin America conference.
He thought the benefits outweighed the harms.

Che turned again to Latin America;
Left his family to fight in the jungles of Bolivia.
Back to the basics, a guerrilla again;
For almost a year, fighting alongside other men.
And Tania, too, an East German woman;
(Born in Argentina of German Jew parents)
A spy uncovered, she joined the fighting;

125

But killed along with most other guerrillas who were dying,
Che's guerrillas were down to seventeen men;
The United States was backing the Bolivians;
They sent the CIA, Special Forces, Rangers with jungle training;
On October eighth Che was wounded and taken.

Che killed the next day on October 9, 1967, age 39;
A Bolivian soldier volunteered and shot him.
Che's hands were cut off for identification;
Lying there like Jesus after crucifixion.
In Bolivia, Che was sacrificed;
Rode a donkey, too, but violent;
Like Christ and the anti-Christ;
A passion to help the down-trodden.

Che said his two greatest weaknesses were reading and cigars;
A less thoughtful man might say women and bars.
We're left with Che's writings, his speeches, his diaries;
His desire for justice, equality and fairness.

Haydee Santamaria the only woman
In every phase of the Cuban revolution.
I can't imagine how she survived;
No wonder she was a suicide.
In jail after Moncada in 1953,
The guards brought her her brother's bleeding eye,
And her fiance's bleeding testicle just before both would die.
She wrote to dead Che and lived and died in Cuba in 1980.

Fidel Cuba's communist dictator until 2008;
Cuba very poor, an economically failed state.
Raul became president, is still today;
Holding on to power, liking to dictate.
Don't know if it's true that Raul's not poor.
Whereas Che wouldn't live in luxury nor drive a nice car,
It's rumored that Raul is worth a hundred million.
Che would roll over in his grave and mourn for the revolution.

Che a doctor, Fidel a lawyer;

Few revolutionaries have ever been smarter.
Batista was bad, they wanted better,
But it's a shame they weren't wiser.

Che Guevara: "And it must be said quite sincerely that in a true revolution, to which everything is given, from which no material returns are expected, the task of the revolutionary vanguard is both magnificent and anxious... In these conditions, a great dose of humanity is needed, a sense of justice and truth, if we are not to fall in the trap of extreme dogmatism, of cold scholasticism or isolation from the masses. Every day you have to fight so that love for humanity can be transformed into concrete deeds, into acts that set an example, that mobilize." (The Che Handbook by Hilda Barrio and Gareth Jenkins, New York: St Martin's Press, 2003, p. 358)

Sources: The Che Handbook; Wikipedia.

The Constitution

A more perfect union
Is what they were thinking;
Blessings of liberty,
Insure domestic tranquility.
Promote the general welfare;
Do some even care?
Provide for defense,
But let's use good sense.

The first ten amendments the Bill of Rights;
They're there for our protections;
We trust their might
Through our democratic elections.
One: Don't promote or prohibit religions;
Press and speech still are freedoms;
Can petition and peacefully protest;
All important like the rest.
Two: The right to bear arms;
A regulated militia to protect from harms.
(But that was before automatic rifles
With many rounds of ammo
And bombs and such; how far do we go?)
Three: Don't take over homes, you soldiers,
Without first getting consent from the owners.
Four: Have reasonable cause to get warrants
To search or seize persons, homes, belongings.
Five: Seems this addresses habeas corpus,
But some say that's the fourth.
I'm not a Constitutional lawyer; I make rhyme;
It limits holding most persons for a crime.
Also, the fifth prevents double jeopardy;
Grants due process, the right to a trial;
Not made to testify against yourself,

Whether you'd tell the truth or a lie.
Six: For crime, a fair and speedy trial is the intent
Are we close to what our fore-father's meant?
Near the site of the crime, have impartial juries,
Can have witnesses for and against, and lawyers
Seven: Common law, civil suits of more than twenty dollars
Can also have final trials by impartial juries.
Eight: Bails or fines can't be too many dollars;
Punishment cannot be cruel or unusual.
(But who's to say what is too many dollars?
To some what's a lot is not to others;
And sometimes punishment has seemed quite unusual;
Some see hangings, electrocutions, injections as cruel.)
Nine: Don't use these rights to deny rights to others,
Or to disparage rights of the people.
Ten: The powers not delegated by the Constitution
Are reserved to the States or to the people.

There's much more I won't list here;
Voting rights, civil rights; THE SLAVES WERE FREE;
Amendment thirteen, then amendment fifteen;
Former slaves could vote, if they were men.
FIFTY YEARS LATER, amendment nineteen
Let women vote if they had reached twenty-one;
FIFTY MORE YEARS, you could vote if eighteen
Due to the draft and much protesting.

The Constitution can be confusing and evolving,
Debated and subject to interpretation;
Yet, we owe so much to it in our nation.
Thank you, founding fathers, for our good foundation.

My Presidents

I barely remember President Truman,
But later I thought it was inhuman
To drop two bombs on cities in Japan,
And do such harm to one's fellow man.
It's complicated, as I live and learn,
For peace and justice don't all still yearn.
But seems it should be much simpler
For there to be no war, especially nuclear;
For there to be no Nazis fighting for Hitler;
And no kamikazes dying for Hirohito;
Brainwashed by his orders from Tokyo.

I remember "I like Ike," a war hero;
And my cousin fighting Communists in Korea.
Didn't think much then about segregation;
Civil rights and Dr King got little of my attention.

Since my family was Republican and Protestant,
And we'd never had a Catholic president;
Though Kennedy gave his assurance,
His Catholic church wouldn't have too much influence;
I pulled for Nixon, but Kennedy won;
And it wouldn't be the last we'd hear of Nixon.
Who wouldn't like Kennedy, so smart and young?
A teenager now, I started paying more attention.
When Kennedy was killed the world was aghast;
We worried when we heard he was going to Dallas;
Yes, we were afraid he'd be shot by racists;
Still some there, in the State of Texas.
I know this sounds really awful to say,
But I suspected Johnson, still do to this day;
Just thought he looked guilty, my intuition;
With the most to gain, the biggest reason.

130

Johnson, to his credit, got the Civil Rights Bill;
And very needed health insurance Medicaid and Medicare.
He had his wars on crime and poverty, the war in Vietnam;
Didn't run in '68; what did Nixon know on him?

Strange how some Nixon has opposed;
How their chapters have oddly closed;
Johnson wasn't shot but Wallace was;
And MLK and RFK, not just JFK in Dallas
Nixon known as "tricky Dick";
Exposed by his own tapes he sneaked;
With his dirty tricks and phony phrases;
His southern strategy appeal to racists.
Nixon spoke of "peace with honor"
About ending the Vietnam War;
The US killed more than a million Vietnamese
While Nixon spoke of honor; Oh pleeeeeeeease!
More than 50,000 of our US troops died;
Agent orange got some later, many still suffer;
But Johnson and Nixon so easily sent them and lied,
And rich corporations got richer and richer.
Anti-war protests helped end the fight,
As civil rights marchers helped gain rights.
Eighteen-year-olds who used to be drafted
Got the right to vote, thanks to activists.
Nixon's war on drugs against hippies
Against his war in Vietnam;
Known for China trip and ping-pong;
For Watergate, impeachment or resign.

Ford seemed nice, not elected but chosen;
May have known more than was known;
Gave Nixon a deal; was on the Warren Commission;
Somehow rose to the highest position.

Carter brought a welcome relief;
A true Christian in his belief;
A moral man after all of the guile;
Smart and kind, with a great big smile;

131

We could finally stop tasting bad bile.
Carter had been a Georgia farmer and governor;
A nuclear engineer, no president smarter;
Annapolis and Georgia Tech grad, a Navy officer;
Now a cancer survivor, an author, still a Sunday school teacher.
Carter was good, a humanitarian, a decent man;
Some say he erred with the former Shah of Iran;
Let him in the US for medical treatment;
Iranians made more than a statement;
Held US hostages 444 days;
Killed no hostages but killed Carter's presidency.
During Carters four years no US troops died in war;
That is the most important fact by far.

I mourned when next a movie actor, not a movie star,
Who was making films during the second world war;
Reagan was from California, the former governor,
Taking pride in being a conservative Republican.
Reagan was likable if you overlook the mean;
Said he wanted government to be small and lean.
One of his first acts was filled with cruelty
College students with a dead or disabled parent lost their Social Security.
Small and lean can't mean the military;
But take the funds from Social Security.
Reagan giving big tax breaks to the wealthy a problem;
When he wasted a lot on his failed "Star Wars" program.

Then Bush 41, Reagan VP and from the CIA;
A silver foot in his mouth, Ann Richards would say.
Gotta give him credit for his World War II service;
Youngest pilot, not a wimp, despite a magazine cover.
Seemed rather harmless; I just sighed;
"No new taxes"; of course he lied.
Talked out of both sides of his mouth;
Later out-talked by a native of the South.
Bush 41 had a war when Iraq invaded Kuwait;
Saddam Hussein's troops saw swift defeat;
Some said Bush 41 shouldn't have stopped Desert Storm
Until his troops had gone to Baghdad and gotten Saddam.

Bush 41 not as nice as he might appear;
Giggled about JFK's death at President Ford's funeral?
Said Bill Clinton only a small southern state governor;
And called Al Gore crazy for trying to save the world.

Then the Clintons and what a mess;
Bill Clinton a flawed political genius;
Fewer women than Kennedy but a womanizer;
First time I heard him, he won me over—and the interviewer.
Clinton lost Congress; now Newt Gingrich his grinch;
Clinton called "The Comeback Kid" for his resilience.
Prison and welfare reform, questionable pardons;
Bad politics trying to appease Republicans.
Somalia, Rwanda, Bosnia, other disasters;
Bin Laden's rise, NAFTA, successes and failures.
Hillary didn't get healthcare, a major failure;
No matter what, people still blame her;
Even when Hillary's the one who got hurt,
Bill got away with more than being a flirt.
On Whitewater their enemies spent millions,
But failed to pin anything on the Clintons.
They tried to impeach him; to a vote it came;
But the Comeback Kid finished at the top of his game.

And here's when I get really disgusted;
The American people would elect Gore I trusted;
His great Earth in the Balance I appreciated and read;
Surely American voters weren't sick in the head.
But the US Supreme Court voted 5 to 4
To end the frustrating Florida vote count;
Taking the presidency away from Gore,
Meaning Bush 43 would become president.

Bush 43 could read books Gore could write;
But Bush 43 was wanting to finish a fight;
He seemed determined to go to Iraq;
And finish the fight his father had lacked.
Oddly to some, Bush 43 chose Cheney for VP;
It seems rather clear, not such a mystery;

133

Cheney had headed Halliburton, its CEO;
A big war contractor, and to war we would go.
Bush 43 and Cheney, for whatever reason,
Ignored the warnings before 9/11;
That day our country would lose about 3,000
In the worst terrorist disaster in our nation.
Seems the attack was planned by Bin Laden with Saudis
Who resented how the US courts rich Saudi royals.
You get our money; you scratch my back;
We get your oil; forget the rights women lack.
Bush 43 was supposedly AWOL from the guard
Years before and didn't have to serve in Vietnam;
Was he working instead on a US Senate campaign
Of Red Blount, a fellow rich Republican?
Blount became Nixon's Postmaster General
(Such people aren't usually an actual general);
He got very rich off of post office contracts;
It helps you get rich when you have such contacts.
Blount would later get the largest contract of its kind
To build the King Saud University in Riyadh;
Another who would build some buildings there
Was Osama bin Laden's rich builder father.
So Bush 43 and Cheney went to war in Afghanistan
Where Osama apparently devised his evil plan;
Helped by Mullah Omar and the Taliban,
Bin Laden escaped and ended up in Pakistan.
But Bush 43 still determined to invade Iraq;
Played on our patriotism, after the 9/11 attack;
Got the votes of Biden and Hillary but not of Barack;
Now most consider the Iraq War a mistake.
Sure, Saddam Hussein needed to go;
Invaded Kuwait, killed the Kurds, this we know;
Had used chemical weapons, a really bad man;
Maybe had weapons of other mass destruction.
But we have reason to not trust Bush 43 and Cheney's intentions,
Or believe what they said about Iraq's worst weapons.
Was this too much about helping rich cronies?
Cheney got millions from Halliburton, which profited billions.
We got rid of Saddam, but at great cost;

Thousands of our US troops' lives were lost;
Many more were wounded; PTSD and many suicides;
Much destruction and hundreds of thousands of Iraqi lives.

If you think we won't pay, then you are a fool;
People don't really follow the Golden Rule;
The lives and the trillions of dollars spent
Are just part of it; there's also revenge.

Then we watched a rising nova;
Believe it or not, named Barack Hussein Obama;
A new US Senator from Illinois;
His father from Kenya; lived in Indonesia and Hawaii;
Half black, half white, all super star;
First time I heard him, I knew he'd go far;
Eloquent and smart, the best speeches ever;
Beat some good opponents, even Hillary.
Hillary was older and had been around more;
And as a woman I was pulling for her;
And, like me as a teen, a Methodist and Goldwater girl;
Until we learned more about the ways of the world.
I was proud of our country election day;
Most important of all I liked Obama's way.
For most it mattered not his name or his story;
Still proud our president could be a man of color.
The national debt with Bush 43 grew from zero to trillions;
Trickle down only helps those with millions.
The world was on the brink of depression;
Instead with Obama we had Bush 43's recession.
Obama bailed out automakers and bankers;
Of course, using money of US taxpayers.
His decisions were difficult; his work was hard;
Though still troubling, he wound down two wars.
We finally got "Obamacare," the ACA,
A national plan finally in the US of A;
Millions more covered, better but flawed;
Again, a phony phrase, not affordable for all.
I love Obama; he was a credit to any race;
And I love how he sang "Amazing Grace."

His wife Michelle, a great first lady,
Who said, "When they go low, we go high";
When mean things we heard would make us cry.
He led with wisdom and dignity and cool and caution,
With a mean Congress and more divided nation.

During Obama's first term Navy Seals killed Bin Laden.
By the end of eight years the national debt nearly 20 trillion.
Seems our leaders always find a way to fund war,
But not through the years to show more care.
You'd think the world's still richest nation
Could do more for healthcare and college education.
After Social Security for college students was ended by Reagan,
It wasn't re-instated by any future Congress or President.
Some of the war debt is owed to Social Security
Borrowing against our retirement future.

It bothered me much, as a female,
That Hillary lost to an unproven male.
In a country with so many bigots and racists,
They'd still prefer Barack Hussein Obama to a feminist.
Hillary the most qualified candidate ever I'm confident
And with millions more votes the last election still not president.
But worst of all Hillary lost to Trump;
He seldom smiles; he looks like a grump;
His eyes look dead; now the top terrorist tool;
He sounds like he didn't learn enough in school.
Yes, now we have Trump, and I'm so ashamed;
When we could have Hillary, but again she is blamed.
Wrongly vilified for decades, blamed for Benghazi;
But Bush 43 ignored the warnings; had more embassy bombings.

Yes, I'm very angry the way things stand;
And that the president is an unfit man.
Women didn't get to vote until 1920;
Let's have a woman president in 2020.

Trump

Trump would win; who would imagine?
We grew up to think that good should win;
That it's wrong to brag and bully and lie;
Or to mock a person's disability.

John Adams was our second president and first VP;
He didn't think much of trumpery;
Fame for fame's sake, egomaniacry;
Now always wanting to be on TV.

Trump threatens torture and nuking, mass deportation;
Banning all Muslims, our new segregation.
He doesn't seem to care about refugees or pollution;
He leads a regressive revolution.

Trump's anti-Christ views leave me in awe
Trump wants to build a Great Trump Wall
To keep out all who are Mexican.
But he can have wives Slovenian and Slovakian;
Marla (daughter of an Elvis imitator) was Southern.
(But her Georgia is now a part of our nation,
Since the Union defeated the Confederation.)

He's uncouth and clueless and a privileged rake;
He talks about bombing Syria and eating cake.
How could anyone vote for such a man
Who brags about grabbing women because he can?

Trump talks about fake news, though he'll often lie;
Says he plays to people's fantasies is the reason why;
Read how he brags about lying in his book,
The Art of the Deal, page 40, take a look.

Trump's a big fraud, with many an empty promise,
He's already bragged and laughed with the GOP Congress
When they voted to end the ACA tax on the wealthy;
They don't seem to care if those they hurt are healthy.

It's hypocritical how some church-goers
Think nothing wrong with Trump, a serial adulterer.
Yet same-sex marriage to them is not right,
But for thrice-married Trump they'd vote and fight.

A leader can be a true hero,
Like Canada's Prime Minister Justin Trudeau;
And Germany's Chancellor Angela Merkel;
Welcoming desperate refugees, unlike Trump the Jerkel.
Trump even insulted Senator McCain for being a POW;
Brags he knows more than our generals; insults our military.

Trump admires Andrew Jackson but doubt he cares;
Does Trump even know about the Trail of Tears?
Trump seems to not know about Frederick Douglass;
I don't think Trump knows enough to be POTUS.
I hate how he talks about Elizabeth Warren;
Calling her "Pocahontas" doesn't help anyone.
Trump lies about, blames, and insults good Obama;
Trump would even stoop to insult your mama.
He would even brag he's greater than Chuck Norris,
When he's really not as great as your uncle Horace.

Trump is unfit and unstable; seems to think conning is cunning;
Fraud Trump recently settled a fraud case for $25 million;
His fraud not considered a crime worthy of a trial and a sentence;
When a poor person who stole or defrauded millions would go to prison.
Trump compares his penthouse to the palace at Versailles
(With his twenty-seven hand-crafted solid marble columns);
Home of let-them-eat-cake Marie Antoinette and Louis the XVI,
Who met their fate by the French guillotine.

Trump pulls out of the Paris Climate Accords,
Deregulates major polluters, a bad hombre;

138

Helps bad bankers, hurts workers and consumers;
We should tell him, "Adios, hasta la vista, au revoir."
Trump makes the country feel we're going off course;
And just when you think Trump can't get worse,
He blames protesters for attacking Nazis and white supremacists;
When everyone should be protesting Trump and such among us;
Too many suffered too much against the Nazis;
And we wonder about Trump's ties with Russia.
We worry even more we'll have nuclear war,
For things are looking bad with North Korea.
Congress should impeach him or use the 25th amendment;
What about our Statue of Liberty and our Constitution?

Right now, this minute, I feel I'm falling apart;
I just saw on TV a scene at a Miami, Florida airport;
A little girl is watching as her pregnant mother sobs over a casket;
It's wrapped with a US flag because it's a soldier;
Sergeant Johnson one of four green berets recently killed in Niger;
From my own son's group based at Fort Bragg;
Trump said to family something like "He knew what he signed up for";
I'm shaking and crying and cursing as I type this,
Cursing awful, disgraceful Trump the POTUS!!!
(Since he was "elected,"
I and many others have been apoplectic.)

Biggest, Fastest, Loudest*

The largest creature known to us yet
Is the blue whale, heavier than a jumbo jet;
At least one has weighed 150 tons (ca 136,000 kg);
The biggest dinosaur about 100 tons (ca 90,000 kg);
The dinosaur on land and about 30 feet (ca 10 m) longer;
Now the blue whale is the animal that's longer.
The African elephant is the largest animal on land;
It can weigh twelve tons and be 20 feet (ca 6 m) long.
The largest reptile is the saltwater crocodile;
It can weigh 3000 pounds (ca 1400 kg) and be nearly 21 feet long.

The largest creature that looks like a spider;
Is an arthropod, not an arachnid, but still scary;
It's the Japanese spider crab, with big long legs;
One weighed 42 pounds (ca 19 kg) and was 12 feet (ca 4 m) long.
And if you think that sounds scary, it only goes south;
In 1991 a 37-foot tapeworm was pulled out of a woman's mouth.
I know I digress, but I must mention the trees;
The giant sequoias in the Sierra Nevada in California
Grow to over 250 feet (ca 80 m) tall, 20 feet in diameter.

Giraffes are now tallest, even their babies aren't small;
Many calves are born six feet (ca 2 m) tall;
Mamas may grow to 14 feet, papas to 18 feet;
In a day they only need less than two hours sleep.
The largest, tallest bird is the common ostrich;
It can weigh nearly 350 pounds (ca 160 kg)
And grow nearly seven feet (over 2 m) tall.
And then there are the men who play basketball;
The tallest have been about seven and a half feet tall.

The fastest animal flies; it's a peregrine falcon;
Flying at over 240 miles (ca 400 km) per hour.
The fastest in the water is a black marlin;
The fastest fish can swim 80 miles (ca 130 km) per hour.
The cheetah is the fastest animal on land;
Can run around 75 miles (ca 120 km) per hour.
The fastest reptile is a central bearded dragon;
It's really a big lizard, like the Komodo dragon;
It can flit or slither 25 miles (ca 40 km) per hour;
Faster than most men, so it we might fear.

Usain Bolt, perhaps the fastest human runner;
With a top speed of nearly 30 miles (ca 45 km) per hour.
Michael Phelps, perhaps the fastest swimmer;
Like Bolt, in the Olympics, swam six miles (ca 10 km) per hour.
Maybe the slowest is the slimy snail;
And maybe the laziest; it can sleep three years.

The loudest land creature is the mighty lion;
They're the only cats that form a pride;
Imagine the noise of a pride of lions and lionesses,
When one can be heard by man for five miles (8 km),
With a roaring noise level of 114 decibels.
The second loudest land creature is the howling wolf,
With a noise level of 90 decibels, more if a pack
The third loudest land creature is the howler monkey;
At nearly 90 decibels, about as loud as the howling wolf;
The howler monkey found in a troop;
It can be heard about 3 miles (ca 5 km) away.

It was once feared that if a plane flew faster than Mach one,
Which is faster than the speed of sound;
At very high altitude flying about 700 (ca 11 km) miles per hour
The plane might disintegrate and worse, no telling;
But brave pilot Chuck Yeager broke the sound barrier in 1947;
Sure there was a sonic boom but not a jet plane explosion.

The loudest creature known is a tiny sea shrimp;
Over 200 decibels, it has its own sonic boom;
Its body, less antenna, only two inches (ca 5 cm) long;
The tiger pistol shrimp it's called, louder than a gun;
Its sonic snap emits tiny light flashes
And brief temperatures nearly as hot as the sun;
If on land or in air there could be an explosion.
The blue whale is the second loudest creature in the ocean;
At 188 decibels, its louder than a jet.

Speaking of jets (I may be the master of segue);
The famous Wright brothers would lead the way.
Their first completed powered airplane flight in 1903;
Flew seven miles (ca 11 km) per hour, and 12 seconds;
For 120 feet (ca 36 m), less than the wingspan of a 747.
The longest chicken flight (or glide) on record was 13 seconds.

Now to the heaviest known people I'll turn:
Seven of the top ten are north American;
The US of course, one Egyptian, one Mexican,
One Saudi Arabian, nine men and one woman;
The largest one from the United States;
A man who weighed 1400 pounds (ca 636 kg);
He's also the one who lost the greatest;
Seems he lost over 900 pounds (over 400 kg).
The heaviest woman weighed 1200 pounds (ca 545 kg).

Now I'm about to finally wind down;
And you might be surprised to know the most toxic toxin;
Although it's injected cosmetically it's botulinum.
Second, no surprise, is viper snake venom.
Seems a doctor in Pittsburgh killed his wife with cyanide;
But cyanide is not in the top five;
That would be arsenic, no one should get it.
Fourth is radioactive poison polonium,
Which about a decade ago killed a Russian;
A former officer of the KGB and FSB (not our FBI);

He was Alexander Litinenko who had fled to England;
He opposed Putin and was sure to die;
Many think Putin had him poisoned.
Number five is common mercury;
In some thermometers, water, soil, no telling where;
I've had it in four fillings since I was a girl.
But, in conclusion, I hope you understand
That the most toxic, biggest, fastest, loudest are the lies of man.

*Source for most details in this poem was Wikipedia, obtained July 23, 2017)

Sexual Harassment

She looked good on paper, appearance and dress;
Inside she was an emotional mess.
Somehow, she was able to hide
That four days before she had tried suicide
When she went for a big job interview;
A good company in town, but no one knew.
Barely 100 pounds; she had lost weight;
Through love and loss, her grief was great.

Her boss hired her over them all;
He weighed over 200, big and tall;
He really liked her and asked her to lunch;
Said her eyes were pretty, a little too much.
A wife and kids but he traveled a lot;
The first time he traveled he stopped by from the airport.
She didn't want to but she opened her door;
She'd never had anything like this happen before.
He had her some flowers that she didn't want;
She told him "You really shouldn't have done that."
She knew she hadn't led him on;
She had no desire; he'd never be the one.
He proceeded to take off her pants;
She said "No" again and again;
Yet he carried her up the stairs
To her bedroom where she felt fears.
She's thankful he stopped his dastardly plan
And never stopped by her apartment again.
She needed her job; thought she could handle it then;
Thought she needed him to think she was his friend.

Once when he was taking a trip most exciting
He said, "You're missing out; you I'd be inviting;
All those sites you'd get to see

144

If you'd go along and sleep with me."
She asked him, "Do you realize
How much you're willing to jeopardize?
What if I went to someone to tell?"
He said, "Who would believe a little divorced female?"

For more than two years most every day,
When he was in the office and not away;
His sexual harassment game he'd play;
He never gave up as long as she stayed.
Until he got a girlfriend, an illicit affair;
Which took a lot of pressure off of her.
He confided his wife was for whom he'd be crying
To be with when he was old and dying.

And now, I'm telling the damnedest thing;
Something she really couldn't explain;
She had moved away to another State;
Her birthday was soon; he wanted to celebrate.
She was half afraid but didn't want to hurt his feelings;
And he had given her a job, and they'd become somewhat friends.
They could talk to one another about most anything;
But as they sat and ate she couldn't stop shaking.
He asked her what was wrong;
She didn't say; the list was still long.
He asked her to his room; he hadn't changed,
Again, she said, "No," and never saw him again.

Bigotry, Racism, and Me

❖❖❖

We had some [n-word] neighbors when I was four;
Yes, I used that awful word;
I no longer use but I did in that world;
Some would argue it was more slang than slur.
Not to deny our Southern ways,
And the carryover from awful slave days;
And the racism, hate, awful crosses that burned;
You'd think through the ages we would have learned.
My parents liked those neighbors and their girls,
But they never crossed each others' doors.
The girls couldn't go to our local school;
Segregation in the South was still the rule.
The Scott girls went to town to the school for the blacks;
They rode in the back of Omar Wiseman's pick-up truck;
Omar, with a business in town, taking a risk;
Ride inside with a white man? Who heard of such?
(Omar's family might have been Jews
Perhaps long ago; no one knew.
Would we have cared? Would some frown
Had it been known in our small Southern town?)
Schools segregated but what about church?
Surely churches wouldn't agree to such.
Why no blacks there? No reason why;
For years and years, as time went by.
Our church organist's long-term maid;
Away from our Methodist church she stayed.
What about Maggie Hayden? I never thought;
But I heard she was barred by the Baptist church vote.
Daddy praised a black man, Maggie's brother Malachi,
For killing the meanest white man around.
He was let out of prison to come home and die.
My family the only whites when they put him in the ground.
I remember the separate water fountains;

No blacks in theaters, diners, lunch counters;
Hotels, hospital rooms, some whole hospitals, too;
Carnegie Hall, Congress, conventions, how cruel.
Even jobs for many blacks were banned;
Perhaps even today, truth be known;
But still blame the black and the poor;
Remember who couldn't walk in the front door.
I remember well the Civil Rights movement
Led by brave Martin Luther King Jr;
But like Einstein, a Jew, Hoover's FBI
Tried to make out he was a Communist spy.
So proud of Kennedy and Johnson, too,
When some found it hard to decide what to do;
Leading the country to do the right thing;
Causing many Dixiecrats to become Republicans.
Why shoot and kill JFK, then MLK and RFK?
All the biggest heroes of our day.
Despite what some may say;
Don't tell me no conspiracy.

More than fifty years now since a bomb
Was set off at a black church in Birmingham;
Killed four girls in church from eleven to fourteen.
How can people be so damned mean?
Yet, I don't remember when I was a girl
Hearing in church any preacher,
Or in class hearing any teacher,
Speak against the wrongs against "people of color."

I suspect my uncle in the KKK,
Or at least went to meetings and heard them say,
"Coretta Scott King was married to JFK";
Still so much ignorance today.
I still remember the ignorant grins
When we heard on TV that King was dead.
How could these people be my family and friends?
Why are they so wrong in the head?
I saw Harry Belafonte on a TV program;
He was so handsome I was admiring him;

147

When my daddy said, "I'd shoot you now
If I thought you'd marry one of them."

When I was a girl I had romantic notions;
Playing in the woods among the laurels;
Pretending I was marrying a handsome Indian;
I still today mourn for and romanticize them.
As it turned out, when I married my husband,
We thought he was likely part native American;
Possibly Cherokee, black hair, eyes brown;
But later learned there was likely some African.
I just thought that he was good looking,
And I would have smart, beautiful children.

So many poor Africans die of deprivation;
Dirty water, disease, and even starvation.
In places with valuable uranium and diamonds
And other rich resources but the poorest nations.
Bad treatment, corruption, exploitation;
Rich or poor face discrimination in our own nation.
And as if that's not enough some get sickle cell,
Which actually protects many from malaria;
But now I wonder, who can tell,
About some who have ancestors from Africa;
If kidney problems aren't caused by a trait of sickle cell?

I heard a woman tell how she left her husband
After he said, "That's the skinniest little [n-word] I've ever seen";
About a little boy dancing his heart out;
I don't blame her for leaving such a lout.

I had never seen a Muslim or a Mexican
Until college, I think, when I would learn
That some people also looked down on them;
When I just thought they were real handsome.

I moved to Montgomery in my thirties;
Still a long way to go in the nineteen eighties;
Saw people who objected to blacks in the room.

To a place in Hell do they belong?
I bumped into George Wallace when shopping one day;
He was governor, in his wheelchair, to my dismay.
When I bumped into him I felt like a dope;
He said, "Bless you, my child," like he was the Pope.
He looked awful, like one who suffers;
Should such a thing happen to such others?
Yes, he was governor again after many years,
After playing on people's racism and fears.
(After his wife Lurleen was Alabama's first female governor
It would be fifty years until they had another.)

I had never been around many a Mexican,
But I fell in love with a "bad-assed Texan";
Turns out he was part Apache Indian;
A bow and gun hunter, a man among men.
I didn't know he was such a Republican;
Recently saw he likes Trump and Jeff Sessions.
("Be careful who you fall for" is one of my lessons.)
I can imagine how it was back when;
"That's worse than a [n-word]!" being an Indian.
He gave me a picture he took of Jimmy Carter
At a bass tournament; then showed me another
Of him with Bush 41 on a boat in the water;
I liked the first one more than the other.

I bought an old house, a real fixer upper;
I was desperate for help, needed good workers.
My heroes were two good hard-working men;
Honest and able, a Mexican and a Puerto Rican.
Once I worked with a man who anything would say;
Who one day could have been shown the door;
After some Hispanics at work walked away
He spoke of the grease he imagined they left on the floor;
A case for not exchanging wisdom
For wit or fun or any bad reason.
Yet he spoke out against the KKK;

Called them silly SOBs right to their face,
As he saw them march and he stopped his car
To the fear and glee of his black passenger.
(Who was our company's EEO officer)

In a civil rights case I became a plaintiff;
The only white person after I witnessed
Blacks who were obviously past twenty-one,
Asked for two IDs while I was asked for none.
The next day I called the ACLU;
A case was building; I was glad they knew.
It took awhile for the case to be won
With two good lawyers, a Jewish man, a black woman.
I've seen some spot blacks in a restaurant
And go out the door; whatever for?
Certainly, they were no better than them;
One table a party with the black mayor of Birmingham.
There's the Southern Poverty Law Center, besides the ACLU,
And others doing great work for civil rights, too.

Sure, some blacks have their problems
With too many shootings and crime;
But a little white-haired old lady
Is guilty, too, when she won't sit down with them.
I've seen more than one, a little old white mother,
Herself a patient at Grady Hospital psych ER;
Treated kindly by largely black staff,
Even after racial epithets spewed from her mouth.
We've all seen bigotry and racism and wrong cop killings;
We've seen it in Charleston and Charlotte and Charlottesville;
And Montgomery and all over and not just the South.
I've also been disappointed to hear a table of black teens
Loudly spewing the n-word and f-word
At the Asheville Mall at the food court.
"I wish that old woman would get away from us,"
One said about me, minding my own business.
Another time in a popular area in Asheville, to my dismay,

Some large black teens were lying on the splash pad that day.
When I asked them why, they just ignored me, so I just walked away;
Mothers with several children in strollers stood there waiting and didn't say.
I'm no Rosa Parks, but I wonder if I could have helped some way.
I've seen the bad, the problems, the hate, crime and crazy;
Good and grace, hard work and study, the love and the lazy;
From white, black, and all, sisters and brothers;
For twenty dollars for crack a man killed his grandmother.

My nephew dated a girl half Asian;
I think my daddy thought it beneath his raising.
When he didn't bring her to the reunion,
Daddy asked "Where's your little Jap Asian?"
I dated a half Asian, half black man;
Best looking guy I thought in Atlanta;
Broke up before he met my soon dead Daddy;
Good because I guess Daddy might have killed me.
Daddy had no reason to feel superior;
His fourth-grade education a little inferior;
If you want to keep such a score;
And Daddy was allowed in the front door.
Mother was humble, usually kind,
But she lashed out at Daddy and life one bad time;
Said "I'm her [n-word]" (of our church organist's daughter);
Her maid, babysitting, cooking and cleaning for her.
[And since I cleaned our house, was I our (n-word)?]

Among all, amazing things we see;
Like the doctor born in North Korea;
Came to the US when she was sixteen;
Went to MIT when she was eighteen;
Like another brilliant doctor, Ben Carson;
From poverty became a famous neurosurgeon;
And then there's Dr Albert Einstein;
And too many to count doctors named -stein;
And many others no matter the race;
It doesn't matter how we look in the face;

Or our religion or not our ethnicity;
Or our learning or not or nationality;
What matters is how we treat others;
Among our diverse sisters and brothers.

I claim to not discriminate,
To treat all the same;
I took a black male roommate;
Master Bates should have been his name;
Late one night a knock on my door in Atlanta;
He said, "I'm M's friend visiting from Toronto."
My housemate M was not yet there;
But I welcomed his friend who went up my stair;
A stranger, a black man, to M's room; it was all right;
I went back to bed and slept through the night.
(Better than when M's sounds came from his cot.)

Had a Korean lover; I guess just for spite;
His ?ex-wife sang opera; his eyes looked like slits;
I shouldn't say such; sounds like bigots.
My long-time crush had a Korean wife;
It seemed unfair; I wanted him in my life;
Then he left the Buddhist and married a Muslim;
He a Catholic deacon, in 2001 before 9/11.
He's now with a new Catholic woman;
This time (like Ed Lansdale) a filipina, oh please;
When another I want married a Chinese.

How could I not also tell this?
If I didn't tell, I'd be remiss.
After 9/11, my last lover a Muslim, not a good one;
He smoked and drank beer and had many women.
He said, "I'll eat anything," beef and pork, too.
Though a Hindu lover said he'd eat neither;
I don't remember about the Jew;
I didn't stay with any of them, either.

We'll remember 9/11, but it was a few men
Who took over planes; caused so much destruction.
When there are millions of Muslims,
A few took the lives of our US three thousand.
After 9/11 I asked my dear friend,
A Muslim who grew up in Pakistan,
"Why do they hate us?"
She tried to explain:
They see the US befriend the rich royal Saudis,
While most of the Saudis have so little.
Hatred and terror from the despair;
One might see that they'd become bitter.
She was a good friend; brought her kids to my pool;
She wore a long leotard; I showed skin;
We shared laughs and notes; it felt very cool;
She settled in Texas; I miss my friend.

Now some wrongly say let's ban all Muslims;
Build a wall to keep out the Mexicans;
Deport them, too, as if they're not human;
Still injustice, too many in prison;
Maybe no lynchings, but still racism.
We've come a long way, a long way to go;
President Obama was just one bro.
He was ridiculed, blocked, obstructed, some lied;
Some wrongly condemned and vilified.
When children were shot he met families and cried;
Sang Amazing Grace at the church where blacks died.
It was 2015, there were nine of them;
Shot down in cold blood after welcoming
A troubled young man into their church home;
His fellow "white supremacists" share the blame.
That church's dear people and families
Were models of goodness for all to see.
They spoke of our shared humanity;
Showed us all how all should be.

153

Some finally, peacefully, took down the flag
That many thought should be a rag;
For it symbolized slavery and oppression,
A wrong civil war, an awful lesson.
(Nikki Haley, why are you a Republican?
And Tim Scott, it's no longer the party of Lincoln.)
Amazing Michelle a great first lady;
The vilification was down-right crazy.
"When they go low, we go high," she said;
With goodness and wisdom the Obamas led.
If black people do well, some say that they're uppity;
All the name calling is a pity and nasty.
I'm sure some I know called trailer park white trash;
So wrong for all this meanness to last.

I know a girl whose husband dragged her out of bed;
That dear girl, by the hair of her head;
Said he dreamed she was "f---ing a [n-word]";
She had the best comeback I think I've ever heard;
In her sweet little voice said, "I dreamed I was too";
Glad she's survived and that marriage is through.

I had a black friend in Atlanta, high yellow, mulatto;
(So many names as if they should matter);
In Atlanta I, white, became a minority;
In age and in race; it was not pretty.
I started to feel that things were not fair;
Feeling so bad and that no one would care.

Last year I watched several episodes
Of Shades of America, a CNN show;
All across our land for stories to tell,
Told by the show's host, Kamau Bell.
He talked with the KKK, who said to his face;
And we heard them say it, to their disgrace,
"It's better to murder than mix our race."
Yes, some think miscegenation, the races mixing,
Is worse than murder, worse than lynching.

Some in the family have mixed race children
Frowned upon by the older generation;
One on his deathbed asked for forgiveness
Because he had treated some grand-children less.

North Carolina has its Lumbee Indians;
Some claim the Lost Colony mixed with Croatans,
Who also mixed with Africans;
Some claim a mixture of tribes and regions.
I say, "Aren't we all just Americans?"
And better yet, "Aren't we all just humans?"

Yet I don't ignore when writing this rhyme
That sure, we have black on black crime,
And all kinds of crime, all races, too;
But shootings still going on in this day and time
For being black, by the men who wear blue.
Sure, cops have hard jobs with danger and stress;
Split-second decisions, but still too many deaths.
Colin Kaepernick decided to stand out from the rest;
And kneel during the national anthem as a form of protest;
To bring greater awareness to a problem
Of police shooting blacks possibly due to racism;
Many questioned Kacpernick's patriotism;
Some opposed and some sided with him.
I say "What better way to honor those who fought fascism;
To honor our country, our flag, all of us;
Than to peacefully protest injustice?"

We no longer have some family and several others
Who speak so sadly about other sisters and brothers;
Who say, "All [non-Christians] and homosexuals should burn in Hell";
Who ridiculed President Barack and First Lady Michelle.

So many are estranged from friends and family
Over differences in race, politics, bigotry;
Where are we headed? How will it end?
When we don't even talk to some family and friends?

Love Girls Boys Trans Queers

I don't care what others say;
There's nothing wrong with being gay;
For love we shouldn't have to fight;
For love we all should have the right.
As for me I'll listen to nature
More than to some hateful preacher;
Preaching some anti-love sermon;
Saying it's wrong to be a loving human.
"Homosexuals should burn in Hell!"
I've heard a radio preacher yell.
Wonder how bad homosexuals must feel?
When some don't see their love is real?

Some men want men;
Some women want women;
Some men want to be women;
Some women want to be men.
Some women want to look like men;
Some men want to look like women;
Some want to love both;
Some want to take the marriage oath;
All want to be loved, like me and you.
"But it's a sin," say some; "against God's rule."
Some pick and choose their sinners and sin;
Think they can marry again and again.
Bomb Iraq and Iran, have a Muslim ban;
Turn away, build a wall, deport a Mexican.
God may or may not be, but LGBTQ love is real.
It's not your place to say they're wrong to feel.
So don't condemn them; don't be cruel.
Just try to remember the Golden Rule.

Leaves of Grass

"Of physiology from top to toe I sing,"
Wrote Whitman in "One's Self I Sing"
In <u>Leaves of Grass</u> (a lengthy thing);
Of marijuana here I sing.
Some choose to fight the EPA
While courts uphold the DEA.
Since 1970 a US crime,
Ranked right there with heroin.
It's *Cannabis sativa*, hemp, THC;
Classed with the worst, a strange legality.
Some people possessing even go to jail;
The laws against it we should repeal.

Food, fuel, cloth, clothes, rope, better plastic, useful stuff;
Paper, paint, insulation, made in France. Are
they smarter than us? (we, oui?)
Much less harm than many worse;
The laws against it are a curse.
Anxiety, cancer and its symptoms, other disease and stress relief;
Nausea, pain, seizures, spasms; help them all is my belief.
It can make you feel silly, feel happy, feel well;
See better, smoked, swallowed, shot, so some tell.

Used by infamous, non-famous, some with fame;
So many names, it's like a game.
Giggle Smoke, Good Giggles, ganja, grass,
Merry Jew Wanna, pot, reefer, tea, hash,
Bammy, Boom, Bobo, Haha Bush,
Donna Juana, Dagga, Ding,
Joy Smoke, Joy Stick, Jolly Green,
Juanita, Aunt Mary, Mary Jane.
Sometimes marijuana is also called dope,
But can also help one keep one's hope.

As for me, I've only smoked four halves;
Felt nothing with two; with two fun and laughs.

Let's have research on marijuana using;
Make sure it's more help than harm to sick children.
If unknown effects are what you fear;
You who think little of other danger;
Like what is happening to our atmosphere;
Like shooting guns and alcohol drinking;
You might need to change how you are thinking;
Think we might need a lot more learning,
When pollution kills 200,000 a year in our country.

Leaves of grass, bags of weed;
Better rope, legal dope, more hope;
Join in and spread the seed;
Legalize everywhere hemp and weed.

Heroin in the World

Heroin and other opiates made from opium;
All opioids made in labs, as are synthetics that are legal;
In the United States heroin is medically illegal;
But is legal with prescription in the United Kingdom.

But whether legal or illegal
These drugs are often lethal;
Over 10,000 US heroin deaths last year;
And ten times as many in the rest of the world.

Two top US heroin towns to my surprise
Are number one Wilmington and Hickory number five;
In North Carolina, to my shock and dismay;
Too close to home, not far from (fictional) Mayberry.

Over half a million addicts in the US on heroin;
Thought mostly from Colombia and Mexico;
In the rest of the world twenty million or so;
From opium from poppies grown in Afghanistan.
You better believe that there are big profits;
Money being made off all these addicts;
So why is Afghanistan so damned poor
When they make most of the heroin in the world?
I'm talking about what is mostly legal;
Medical diamorphine, used in Europe, Asia, Australia;
It doesn't add up; where's the money going?
Without a doubt there's lots of corruption.
While most of Afghanistan's people are poor;
And heroin addicts ask for more, more, more;
They develop tolerance to feed their euphoria;
And people make a profit while others suffer.
In Afghanistan one in ten children will die by age five;
Only in South Sudan do more new mothers die;

Three-fourths of the women have no formal education;
Yes, why is Afghanistan such a poor nation?
More than a third of Afghanis don't have a job;
And more than that make less than a dollar a day;
The money's going somewhere, but the people are robbed;
It's all mess up; people should do better, I say.
Wish it was as simple as "Just say no";
Or "Do the right thing" as slogans go.
Everyone knows that heroin here is illegal,
And everyone knows that it's often fatal.

It sometimes starts with chronic pain;
But sometimes starts with just a fling;
Thinking one will try some new thing;
Maybe with a friend to try to fit in.

And corruption is wrong, like in Afghanistan;
Or part of a Colombian or Mexican drug ring;
And bad to deal drugs in a US gang;
In the wild, wild West such people would hang.
From the lowest dealer to the highest seller;
On some level you're something of a killer.
I happen to think we should be better;
Wouldn't it be better to be a helper?
Some doctors and drug companies are guilty, too;
They may over-prescribe and make a profit;
And sometimes cause or enable the addict;
Who then turns to heroin to make it through.
I'm sorry for those with chronic pain,
And I know it's not really always simple.
But what is wrong with some of you people?
Heroin is bad, for sure; USE YOUR BRAIN!!

Side Effects

Many medicines save lives without a doubt;
But some of the side effects we can do without;
Besides the widespread epidemic
Of drug abuse and narcotics addicts;
With death being one of the side effects;
Non-prescription drugs can reduce pain;
Overuse can cause fatal bleeding;
Even a drug seemingly harmless like aspirin.
What about four hours of priapism?
Or lack of production of calcium?
Some drugs save the kidneys from hypertension,
And the brain from strokes; too many to mention.
Some drugs damage the kidneys and liver;
Some increase risk-taking behavior;
Can cause eventual sleep deprivation;
Like some drugs given for hyperaction.
Or reduction over time in cognitive function
And movement disorders with drugs for psychosis.
Another problem controlled but pulmonary fibrosis.
Nausea bad and hair loss a minor problem
If your life is saved by your treatment.
But be aware and question your medicine.

It Can't Be Done

Some said "It can't be done,"
But starting in 1875
Some dared to run the railroad
Through the Eastern Continental Divide.
In North Carolina the mountains too high
For a train to climb to the land of the sky.
"Build some tunnels," someone would say;
Adding twists and turns, they found a way.
From the county of McDowell to Buncombe
The railroad they would welcome;
The most earth moved at the time in the USA;
No greater railroad challenge here ever faced.

It was only ten years after the Civil War;
Lacking funds, the State was poor;
Not enough money to buy black powder;
They decided to use convict labor.
First they had to build stockades and such things;
Housing for the convicts, kitchens for their rations;
Some who had helped build their Central Prison
Came from Raleigh to their prison at the mountain.
Unpaid convicts and paid local foremen;
A few black women to work in the kitchen;
One convict count was about 500 black men;
About 20 black women, and 35 white men.
We don't even know any convicts' names;
And we sure don't know about their crimes.
Most were likely former slaves, given the times;
Doubt they were all guilty, more southern shames.

From daylight to dark the work was hard;
Breaking into rock, hauling it out by cart;
Clearing trees and dirt and land;

Picks, shovels, sledge hammers, flat rocks by hand.
Fire and cold water used to crack rock;
Then the idea to lay track;
And use a locomotive many men would pull
To pull the carts when they were full.

Major James Wilson, project head, bought nitroglycerine;
So they learned to use this new Nobel invention.
It may have added to the dangers;
No telling how many deaths and injuries.

Six total tunnels formed in all;
Each would be fifteen feet tall.
The shortest one was 89 feet long;
The largest, 1800 feet, was Swannanoa Tunnel.
For the trains to climb 1000 feet,
With curves that would equal nearly 3000 degrees;
The track would curve over nine long miles,
Though only 3.4 miles as the crow flies.
Swannanoa Tunnel an amazing feat,
When two crews on each end managed to meet
On March 11, 1879 right in the middle;
Meeting like that was quite incredible.

The railroad's still there, tunnels and all;
A popular site, especially in the fall.
If you're on I-40 in your car,
And near Old Fort, it's not very far.
Take the short road to Andrew's geyser.
You can see where the railroad starts to get higher,
And starts to wind for the trains to climb;
And better yet take an excursion train ride.

You'll see no worker statues or monuments;
Doubt there were pardons and proclamations;
Heard of no medal or award;
No Nobel prize, just our pride and their labor.

*This poem based on the book TUNNELS, NITRO AND CONVICTS: Building the Railroad That Couldn't Be Built by Stephen R. Little, Bloomington IN: AuthorHouse, 2010, 36 pages. Steve Little is mayor of Marion, North Carolina in McDowell County. He also has a children's book and is working on a full-length book about building the railroad tunnels. He gives talks on the subject (can view on YouTube) and has been known to break down and cry when he talks about the plight of the convicts. He is a very good man and mayor.

Ella May Wiggins

Ella May born in Cherokee County, North Carolina
to James and Elizabeth Maples May;
Her father killed when she was a young black girl
on his lumberjack job one fateful day.
She went to work in a textile mill where she met
Johnny Wiggins and married him;
They left the mountains, and in ten years there were seven more of them.
They moved to Gaston County, but Johnny
left after she bore seven children;
Two of them died of respiratory infection and rickets and malnutrition.
She had to go to work in a textile mill, about 70 hours for $9 a week.
Gaston County was the major textile center of the entire South.
The industry was stressed, the economy getting more bleak;
Workers were laid off, and those who worked
suffered and didn't make enough.
Ella May, like many, joined the Communist
National Textile Workers Union,
And arose as a capable leader bringing in others
near her home in Stumptown.
There was a large strike and an angry mob tore
down the NTWU headquarters;
And Ella May found out someone had poisoned
the spring she used for water.
Ella May saw the Union as her only hope and said so in ballads;
Like in "The Mill Mother's Lament" she wrote and sang so sadly:
"While we slave for the bosses,
Our children scream and cry."
But she and her voice stood strong despite all her losses,
And she would continue to lead and try and try.
Soon after, tensions were getting greater in June 1929;

Deputies broke up a union rally and men,
women and children in a picket line.
Much division, with many against the union, many for the union rooting;
That night a unionist and four policemen were wounded in a shooting;
And the Gastonia chief of police was shot and killed;
Over 70 union members were arrested and jailed;
After a week all but 16 were released;
The trial moved to nearby Charlotte where the case was dismissed;
Anti-union mobs again destroyed Gaston union
halls; so many were distressed;
On September 10 a mob raided the Charlotte office
of the International Labor Defense.
The NTW Union called for a protest rally near
Gastonia on September 14, 1929;
The anti-union forces had new armed deputies
and vigilantes and hundreds of men.
Ella May was in a group of 22 union members,
sympathizers and strikers with no weapons;
Her group had been turned away from the rally
where she was to speak and sing;
Instead they were pursued, and she appears to have been targeted for killing
By those who didn't like communism or unions or the races mixing;
Two other strikers were wounded, and five men
were indicted for the shootings
When Governor Gardner ordered an investigation
due to Gaston County's inaction;
The men were acquitted in a trial in Charlotte
in 1930, despite 55 eye-witnessing.
Ella May was pregnant when she died and left
five children from ages one to eleven;
They were placed in an orphanage where they took her maiden name May
Due to awful threats made to them after that awful fateful day.
Ella May Wiggins is known as North Carolina's most famous folk heroine.
She died at age 29 about a month before the Wall Street crash in 1929.
Frank P Graham, the president of the University of North Carolina
Made a wise statement about her that today is a needed reminder;

He wrote, "Her death is, in a sense, upon the heads of us all."
For when injustice endangers one of us, it endangers us all.
He saw "not her mistaken Communism, but her genuine Americanism."
Yes, peacefully protesting injustice is the purest
form of American patriotism.

From https://www.ncpedia.org/biography/wiggins-ella; obtained October 17, 2017

Mayhem in Marion

※※⟨⊗⟩※※

On October 2, 1929 about a mile from where I now live
There was a terrible tragedy at a big cotton mill.
It was about three weeks after striker Ella May Wiggins was killed
And about three weeks before the stock market crashed.
Lawmen opened fire in what is called "the Marion Massacre."*
(also the title of a song about it by Woody Guthrie*)
The law had guns, some strikers sticks and stones;
More than twenty-five workers shot, six died of their wounds.
About 600 had been striking for about four months,
Wanting better pay and better working conditions.
Long hours and low pay, tired of being held down.
Mill owners owned many workers' homes in that part of town.
There were rumors of outside agitators, maybe even communists;
And outsiders in small towns are often viewed with suspicions.
It seems the union organizers weren't keen on communism,
And turned to a more moderate union to help them.
Still tensions came to a head and left six people dead.
People were divided, even in the churches;
And no church would hold services for the slain workers.
They didn't cotton to activists and instigators.
Guess they forgot about our founding fathers.
People were purged from their church, a big part of their life,
As if trouble on the job was not enough strife.
People lost their jobs and homes and more,
And many owed debts to the company store.
Many reporters came; it made national news;
The biggest name who came was Sinclair Lewis.
The governor called for the National Guard.
The sheriff and eight deputies with murder were charged.
The rich mill owners paid for a big legal team,
Made of a future governor and state supreme court justice.
A jury in a nearby town acquitted them.
So much for voting for your own interest.

Juries seem to side, right or wrong, with law and order,
And guess one shouldn't judge if one was not there.
Still many were wounded and six people died;
Some town folk had loved ones on either side.
Two workers were convicted of starting a riot.
Maybe someone said, "Let's get those scabs" passing a picket;
And there was something about someone planting dynamite.
The news died down; people didn't want to talk about it;
And over the years the event became a town secret.

*The Marion Massacre is also a book authored by Mike Lawing

Praise to Workers

Perhaps the greatest praise of all
Should go to the hard-working men and women
Working to raise the next generation;
And our forefathers and mothers who made it all possible.
If you're lucky it's a labor of love;
Little praise for those on Earth; more for God above;
Parents who get up during the night;
Soldiers who are willing to fight a good fight;
Those fighting many ways for justice
Are among those to be praised among us.
Firemen, guards, marines, sailors, soldiers;
Police and patrolmen, other law enforcement officers;
The ditch diggers, the drivers, the dentists, the doctors;
The nurses, assistants, elderly and child-care workers;
The truckers, the teachers, their helpers, the principals;
The artists and actors, the entertaining guys and gals;
Social workers, psychologists, other mental health workers;
Miners, chemists, pharmacists, all kinds of therapists;
Jurors and judges and lawyers, the jurists;
Janitors, jokers, pundits, writers and reporters;
Ambassadors and diplomats and mediators;
Those who work on computers to refrigerators;
Brick layers, electricians, plumbers, all building builders.
City councilmen, county commissioners, city mayors;
Those who make a house a home;
Those who adventure and discover and explore and roam.
Those who build our bridges and roads;
Those who carry the heaviest loads.
Those who sit all hours in a factory or on their feet,
And the same job repeat and repeat and repeat.
When I look all around, whatever I see,
I think of the workers who make life easy.
I'm often in awe of their work in many ways;

Vehicles, ships, skyscrapers, trains and railways;
The castles and cathedrals, Earth's man-made wonders;
Engineers, inventors, scientists, technicians, lab workers;
Miners, mechanics, machinists, all kinds of laborers;
Farmers and fishermen, those who feed us the most;
And those who keep air and water safe from coast to coast.
Entrepreneurs, businessmen, bankers if honest and good;
And humanitarians and helpers and donators of food.
Again, those speaking for justice their voices raise;
And all others among us who make it all work;
But those who deserve much more respect and praise
Are those who get very tired and sweat when they work.

Preachers

Preachers can woo and win us one way or others;
Using sin and God himself if we're believers;
With comforting passages, reading a psalm;
Soothing stories and allegories giving us calm;
With truths and lies and threats and promises,
And hopes and dreams of all our wishes.

The first preachers I remember were Baptists;
And though I was young I knew some were ridiculous,
When they said there was something wrong about Elvis
And wearing the latest fad, those blue jean pants.
And when one preached my Grandpa to Hell,
I was eight, but I thought he was crazy as Hell.
Grandpa told jokes; he was funny and kind;
Some jokes about preachers; this preacher was mean.

But none perhaps as mean as Friar Girolamo Savonarola
(Aside from those who would burn doubters at the stake,
Like those who didn't believe in a talking snake);
Who fanatically ruled Florence, Italy as a theocracy for four years.
Life in Florence for many in those years was very dire;
Books were burned in "bonfires of the vanities," with many fears;
But when the tide turned, Savonarola's "reign of terror" was over,
And he was hanged and his own body burned in a bonfire.

Daddy, too, had his doubts about preachers.
As a boy he hated how they came for Sunday dinner.
They'd eat all the chicken, leave none for the children.
Daddy shaved his head once when the bald preacher was eating.
Daddy got worse and couldn't whisper as he got senile;
Asked me for change for five dollars for the collection, with guile.
Or shall I say his manners went down south,
When he said, "I wish that preacher would shut his damned mouth."

The preacher of one local church, I learned,
Cussed like a sailor about his own son.
Asked a grieving orphaned heiress for some of her money;
As a manager at work he fought against the union.
His church filled with racists and anti-gays,
Voted to ban black people with their sinful ways.
The only black person around, a local maid,
His hateful church her presence forbade.
She was one dear woman, wanting to go to church,
Yet banned from church for being black.
But what about "judge not" and the Golden Rule?
What about them? Makes my blood boil!

Punish generations, like the Bible says,
Used to justify some awful ways;
Like the Holocaust, because the Jews killed Jesus;
And used to punish dissidents in North Korea;
Or maybe the church is being punished, too,
For not following the Golden Rule;
A deacon left his wife for the homosexual pastor;
Another married deacon made another preacher's wife a mother.
Often music a big part of the service;
Sometimes the preacher takes up with the organist.
God help us if preachers are the best among us,
For we know that many of them are sinners.
Like Jimmy Swaggart on over 3000 stations
Around the world in many nations.
From the Assemblies of God he was defrocked,
But he managed to make a big comeback.
Reminds me of a story about Rev Terry Praytell;
It's just too ironic for me to not tell;
When my ex-boyfriend told me I'd go to Hell.
The head honcho of a religious majority,
And the founder of a religious university,
Was coming to town to perform the wedding
Of a groom who had an ex-wife and small children.
The bride the daughter of Praytell's fellow rich Republican

And a friend of my ex-boyfriend Nay,
Who was writing a piece on marriage for Rev Praytell to say.
Nay nearly had a heart attack as he wrote,
When I asked him if he'd heard Rev Praytell had sunk,
When walking on water, he got hit by a motorboat.
Was Nay possibly writing for Rev Praytell while drunk?
Nay, he sure knew something about marriage and life;
He broke up with me the week before Valentine's Day;
And before February was over Nay married his fifth wife;
Watch how lovers act around Valentine's, I say.

I was pleased to hear an ex-preacher lover's explanation
About one Sunday when he was in a congregation,
He defended the Kennedys from the preacher's condemnation.
Saying all their family disasters and assassinations
Were punishment for their sins, an awful accusation.

At a big, beautiful church where I used to attend
The preacher stood in the pulpit and said he couldn't understand
Why women could support Bill Clinton, the President.
"Because his sins are less than those of some others," I explained.
And the good work he does outweighs the sin.

As a girl growing up I admired Billy Graham;
He was one of the best, a gifted human.
I heard he wouldn't segregate his congregation
At his crusades around the world and the nation.
I heard he gave money for Martin Luther King's bail
One time for protesting when he was sent to jail.
Billy saved many souls and had decisive wisdom;
But what did he say about Jews when talking with Nixon?

Martin Luther King Jr among the greatest
With his great sermons and speeches and leading protests.
King Sr also a preacher at an Atlanta church when Jr was a boy.
MLK Jr entered Morehouse at fifteen; at Boston U got a PhD in theology.
MLK Jr a preacher leading the bus boycotts in Montgomery;

Led marches in Selma, in Washington, and other locations;
Working hard to fulfill his "I Have a Dream" speech visions.
Such a shame he was killed in Memphis at age 39,
Leaving behind a widow and four young children,
And those who admire him, likely more than a billion.
Yet, I can't remember any other preacher I heard in the days of segregation
Ever speak about racial injustice to any congregation.

Now Billy Graham's son Franklin a different face,
Like many preachers, a fundamentalist evangelist,
With their fight against LGBTs, Muslims and sinners,
But praising anti-Christlike Trump and such awful winners.
What about how hard it is for a rich man to get into Heaven?
(Especially one who bragged about having more than a billion;
And bragged about getting away with grabbing women).
Franklin, what about when Trump mocked a disabled man?
Did you all preach to any voters that such things were wrong?
Franklin had a fit when liberal Duke Chapel went too far;
Was going to ring their bells for Muslim call to prayer.
But Franklin Graham has Samaritan's Purse;
There's good and bad among the pious.
Yes, we have some good Samaritans,
Willing to reach out their kind and good hands;
Open a clinic, feed the hungry,
Help the down-trodden, the sick, the angry.

The Obamas used to attend preacher Jeremiah Wright's church;
A preacher who said such things as, "God damn America";
I don't judge Rev Wright for that; he's been through much;
And for saying folks cling to their "God and guns" I don't judge Obama;
He's just pointing out the hypocrisy of people like some in the NRA;
When we still have too many guns and hate groups in the USA.
Some preach lies against Obama, say he's a terrorist and Muslim;
Says he's plotting a shadow government to do us harm.
Was that Fox so-called News with such lying and distortion?
Afraid it was really coming from a preacher's sermon.

Last time I was at a relative's, maybe forever,
She and her husband were listening to a radio preacher;
Saying, "All [non-Christians] and homosexuals should burn in Hell."
They agreed; I didn't; I no longer see her.
All along I thought my relative who was sitting near me,
When Preacher Parker preached good grandpa straight to Hell,
Didn't believe in such an awful thing as Hell either;
Surprised to hear that she was such a believer.
Last time I went to church, maybe forever,
It was at a children's Christmas Eve service;
Sweet Jesus' birth the children would tell;
Then the preacher had to say "burn in Hell."
It was at that church where I heard a preacher say
That women have a natural desire to go naked;
When after driving to work one cold winter day,
He saw a woman jogging and wearing SHORT SHORTS!
Yes, he said it in a real loud voice
Like some preachers sometimes do for emphasis.
Preachers cause some women to not wear pants
And to not cut their hair because of such rants.
The preacher said that in their congregation
On one side should be women, the other side men;
And a woman should never be president;
And since you should obey your master if you are a servant,
You should obey your boss man if you are a worker.
What if he or she asks you to do something wrong?
What if you need worker protections and a union?
Good preachers will defend what's right and join in.

Pope Francis possibly the best Catholic pope,
Saying great things and giving us hope.
How does anyone explain all those Catholic priests
Who'd preach from the pulpit and then some molest?
And why can't their priests be married men?
And why aren't any of their priests yet women?
There's a paucity of preachers who are women
Perhaps mostly due to 1st Corinthians;

Chapter 14:34&35 call for women in church to be silent.
That's something I love about Episcopalians;
Their priests can be men and women, gays and lesbians.
And Duke Chapel for more than a decade has had same-sex weddings;
Though many churches don't allow them, or even if you're divorced;
Though many preachers and church member are adulterers, of course.

And not just adulterers, some preachers are fake,
Not just breaking the vows that they take;
The funniest such case I've ever known
Was when a wedding was planned; the bride had her white gown.
The preacher found out the groom was divorced,
And being a Baptist, he wouldn't perform the service.
The groom, being something of a character,
Thought up a plan--to get a local theater actor.
He went to the actor's day job and asked, "Will you marry me?"
The look on the actor's face must have been a sight to see.
I'm imagining he replied, "But I'm not even gay";
He must have thought the groom was cray-cray.
I don't really know all the rest,
But I'm imagining he said since they're kin it would be incest.
Anyway, the non-preacher actor cousin came around,
And acted as the preacher as the bride came down the aisle in her gown.

I find it strange how some pick and choose sin.
One of my best lessons about the sin of omission.
I learned it from a teacher who heard it from a preacher.
I don't claim certainty of many a thing
Preachers say is the Gospel of God the Father
(or Allah or Mohammad, or Jesus, either);
In fact, I'm not really a supernatural believer.
But Jesus, real or not, did some great teaching,
And his Sermon on the Mount was great preaching;
But many preachers don't preach about it much
In a wide variety of types of church;
Or demand it appear with the Ten Commandments
On places like government buildings and monuments.

Maybe replace "In God we Trust" on money and cars
With "Blessed are the merciful...the meek...the pure in heart."
Or maybe since the first amendment of the Constitution
Grants our countrymen freedom of religion;
Leave religious slogans off government places;
And people hear preachers in the place of their choice;
Maybe hear more preaching of the Golden Rule;
Do unto others as you'd have them do unto you;
I don't hear all of you, and maybe some of you do;
All you teachers and preachers trying to get through.
Finally, thanks to all the good and great teachers,
And praise, too, to all the good and great preachers.

Prostitutes and Johns

Remember, for every prostitute there's more than one john;
But somehow people seem to condemn the woman.
Of course, some prostitutes can also be men;
But throughout history we mostly think of women,
Working in what's said to be the oldest profession.

A prostitute is often a victim.
So, try to think before you judge them.
Victims of all sorts of desperation,
Just finding a way to make a living.
Sometimes meet men like Jack-the-Ripper;
Rarely a Xaviera Hollander, The Happy Hooker.
Scarlot Harlot coined the title "sex worker";
For it's a job, often dangerous and hard;
With disease, distress, dread, making them tired.
Often prostitutes feel like they will vomit
When a man stinks, is mean, or is very unfit.

Kings have had them, called courtesans,
These higher whores of prostitution;
Submissive but some dominate in a fashion.
Henry VIII, even with all his wives, had Karan.
With King Francis of France, Karan he'd share;
Francis called her "The English Mare."
And Louis XV of France had Madame du Barry.
Princesse de Caraman-Chimay wasn't really European
Nor a princess; her father was a Michigan lumberman.
Chica da Silva was a sex slave in the court in Brazil.
Many others of the rich and powerful
Have turned to prostitutes for their appetites sexual;
To those working alone or those in a brothel,
And whatever other bacchanalia;
From Roman times and before, to the modern era.

The Bible has its prostitutes, too,
And whether or not it's really true
The Bible said God made Hosea marry a prostitute;
Gomer her name before Hosea became Joshua.
Then in Jericho Joshua got help from a whore.
Rahab gave shelter to the Israelites.
Then the walls fell down with their marching might.
And God made the day longer so they could fight;
And the Israelites saved Rahab by the time it was night.
Maybe even Jesus and Mary Magdalene;
But likely not true, maybe blaspheme.
It's said Jesus cast out her seven demons,
And that she was at his crucifixion;
And at his first resurrection appearance;
And that Jesus loved her more than any other disciple;
But hard to believe all it says in the Bible.

Spies have exploited man's sexual nature;
Like Mati Hari in World War I Germany.
And many more who were undercover;
No telling how many secrets men gave away.

There's Air Force Amy who works in a Nevada cathouse.
And the wild, wild west had its whores of course.
Even Calamity Jane sold her favors to men;
Like Shady Sadie to Wyatt Earp in Tucson.
Which reminds me of a former lover,
Whose Texas brothers took him to a bordello across the border;
Their custom, a Mexican whore for their first sexual encounter.

Then there was Daddy's cousin Lucy May,
Who moved to Nevada after divorce and disgrace.
It was the 1940s with little choice,
When a fallen woman had even less voice.
She visited us once and made quite an impression;
She was made up pretty and was sweet and charming.
She praised my daddy and called him honey;
Tho' he wasn't that much and didn't have money.
The way he ate it up was kinda funny.

I was about nine but could recognize
The reason why Mother rolled her eyes.

Lucy May died of apparent cervical cancer, like many women back then;
Like my grandma's mother who had four children with four men.
A definite downside is venereal disease,
Like chlamydia, gonorrhea, syphilis, hepatitis, herpes, HPV, HIV.

I think the first time I heard the word "whore"
Was in the 50s when a woman I knew was getting a divorce.
My parents called her a whore one day;
I cried, "Don't talk about [that woman] that way!"
She would later laugh and say, "No, I gave it away."
A mean boy in school a few years later
Said, "You're a little whore, just like her."
I had never been kissed and certainly not more,
And I'd be a virgin four more years and never a whore.

A madam of multiple brothels in Ohio was Lizzie Lape.
Wonder how many of them covered up rape?
Making women do things they didn't want to do;
And when you're a prostitute you can't prosecute or sue.
Some madams and prostitutes became rather well-to-do;
As the "Golden Heels Madamme" down in Tijuana;
Down came US politicians from California.
And the Mayflower Madam in Washington
Had a little black book with the names of many well-known.
Sometimes johns have their downfalls, sometimes brief;
And while whores get arrested, many johns go free;
Like many a politician and other men.
Some fall down and get up again;
Like Eliot Spitzer and Charlie Sheen.
Eliot Spitzer, New York Attorney General and Governor;
Linked with a call girl, an escort, a "high-class" whore;
Like courtesans serving johns around the world.
Eliot Spitzer, after his sin, had a TV show on CNN;
Charlie Sheen starred in Two-and-a-Half Men,
And laughed and bragged about how he was winning.
Did he know he had HIV and felt like crying then?

Let's not forget preacher Jimmy Swaggart and others
Of those of the cloth, clerical sisters and brothers.
Swaggart was exposed (I don't mean to be rude);
When he was defrocked that doesn't mean he was nude.
He said he was sorry; we watched him cry;
And he made a big comeback by-and-by.
You can forgive and forget that he was linked with whores,
And take his on-line Jimmy Swaggart Bible College course.

And then there are some prostitutes' pimps;
Sometimes protectors from greater risk;
Sometimes more like sex-slave owners;
Often abusers, users, exploiters,
Of under-age, any age, any sex, even St Nick!

Fiction has its whoring dandies quite randy,
And its whores with names like Fanny and Candy,
And Victor Hugo's Fantine in Les Miserables.
Then there are the fictional belles;
Belle de Jour the nom de plume
Of Secret Diary of a Call Girl, by a blogger and scientist.
And Belle in Ah, Wilderness! And Bella in Ulysses.
And who could forget Rhett's Belle in Gone with the Wind?
Reminds me of the whore in Dolly Parton's hometown.

There's the Whore of Babylon, the whores of myth;
The whores of Dionysus and ancient Rome and Greece.
Aztecs have the goddess Xochiquetzal;
The English Agatha and Alexandra of the Irish Celts.
And just when you think you've heard all to tell;
You hear that Saint Nicholas sold his daughters to a brothel.
And there's a prostitute older than 85; how is that possible?
When it's more often much younger women
Who lie with and marry for money much older men.

Call girls, courtesans, escorts, johns, madams, whores, prostitutes;
Bordellos, brothels, cathouses, houses of ill repute.
Now let's get down to the real brass tacks.
Now let's address the obvious facts.

182

Now we come down to the other whores;
Who lie for and work for bad people with power;
Who enable egomania calling for more and more.
And the media whores many seem to adore.
Those who sell their hearts and their souls
For those who play really bad roles.
Not just men and women of the night in whore houses;
Also in Congress, county commissions, city councils, courthouses.
With lying, cheating, harassment and disinformation,
In bedrooms, boardrooms, and offices across our nation;
Selling their souls, claiming fake is true and true is fake,
While bribes and big campaign money and salaries some take.
Is the White House even sometimes a house of ill repute?
And Congress, too, with more than one male and female prostitute?
Maybe I should change to "Prostitutes and Johns and Cons and Dons"
The title of this poem "Prostitutes and Johns."

*Source for most is Wikipedia, obtained August 9, 2017

The Whippoorwill

꧁ꕤ꧂

The saddest song I ever heard
Was sung about a lonesome bird;*
Or was it "He Stopped Loving Her Today"?
So much grief, so much pain, anyway.
I learned about a tragedy,
Not to a human, not to me;
But about a whippoorwill,
And how, they too, may sadly feel.**
She flew into a moving truck;
Did she survive? No such luck.
The farmer found her dead in tatters;
Shall we believe a bird's life matters?
The farmer began to think it's true;
When he went out toward him flew
Perhaps her mate on the attack;
For days and days kept coming back.
The farmer saw the solo mate
Another time upon the gate,
Calling shrilly, causing fright;
Getting scarier, night by night.
In a tree by the door;
Swooping in anger, flying away;
Back again another day.
On the roof, calling for more;
A whippoorwill chorus, coming closer.
Then at the window, in fury and pain;
When will this madness ever end?
Spring after spring the choir was gone;
But a forlorn whippoorwill still heard to mourn.

*"I'm So Lonesome I Could Cry" by Hank Williams Sr
**From a story in the book <u>Country Cured</u> by Jerry Bledsoe, Longstreet Press,
Atlanta, GA, 1989, pp 101-103.

I Killed a Possum and Cried

I killed a possum and cried.
At sixteen, my first road kill;
Yes, I was sad it died;
Didn't see it as I crossed that hill.

I ate meat; I do still;
But lots of thoughts as to the kill;
Of eating game, both big and small;
However killed; I think of all.
Our shoat was just a little pig
When she ran to Daddy's arms away from our dog;
Her trusting eyes were full of fright;
I saw them later; couldn't take a bite.
Went one evening to woods so near
To help my daddy drag out a deer;
A doe, no less, and big brown-eyed;
I see them still; couldn't eat a bite.
I cooked some steak from Sally the cow;
But couldn't eat any; I think of her now.
But sometimes I'm a hypocrite;
I'll enjoy eating meat and not think of it.
In the woods, on safari, or on the farm;
It matters not, they feel the harm.

Some let dogs die for sport and such;
A form of fun, which I don't think much;
And roosters, too, and men, you know;
In war and peace, with a half-time show.
Michael Vick, was he worse than the others?
Who run and tackle their much-watched brothers?
Or us who eat meat, or delight in the slam?
Even if we won't touch a steak or ham?

185

We shudder to think of the animal slaughter;
But what goes on before the act?
Have no doubt it's crowded and awful;
But let's hide and ignore the not-fun fact.
But hunting is fun and gives us food.
The question is, is it really good?
It may be OK if there's really a need,
But is it OK if it's fun and greed?

Driving in My Car

I could hardly wait to drive a car;
Little did I dream I'd drive so far;
A young teen with all that power,
As I pressed the clutch and changed the gear.
It was the days of the mighty GTO,
Corvette, Thunderbird, Mustang, Camaro;
And those were just the American car;
I didn't dream of a Mercedes or a Rolls or a Jaguar;
And doubt I'd heard of a Lamborghini or Ferrari.

I always loved being behind the wheel;
My grandmothers never felt what I would feel,
For I was only in the second female generation
In my family to drive a car in Henry Ford's nation.
My mother learned to drive in her forties;
I couldn't see why she was so nervous;
She had to learn to drive to take Daddy to the doctor;
I couldn't wait to be old enough to take over.
Mother got to church early, confidence she'd lack;
So she could have room in the parking lot
To find a space where she wouldn't have to back;
Me, I'd park parallel, wherever, in any old spot.
Mother never drove from home more than twenty miles,
But she drove to work until she was seventy-five;
Gluing soles in a factory on shoes and boots;
First gluing our souls, giving us roots.

The only time I didn't want to drive
Was when Daddy got drunk and he would ride;
I had to drive him to the liquor store;
Back in my room, I slammed the door.

A red '66 Mustang was my first car;
Brand new with 289 horsepower.
My grandpas had horsepower, too;
Before cars or trucks anyone knew.
Mine was $2500 with a motor but no AC;
For them left was haw, right was gee.
An eighteen-year old with a new husband and a new car;
I drove a little too fast sometimes; I loved the power;
Drove our Mustang to go to a university;
Had only four small accidents, very lucky.
Twice a rock hit my windshield; twice a car hit mine;
The rocks shattered my windshield each time I was driving.
When one rock hit I was pregnant and pulled over and cried.
Both times women drivers hit me and both times they lied.
We drove the Mustang to the hospital when I was in labor,
And came home in it with the new baby.
When we had the Mustang she was too young to remember,
But her first car was another Mustang that was similar.

Some people say others can't drive on snow and ice;
As if one can totally control where they are going.
I know the most scared driving I ever was;
I was driving to Asheville, and at the top of the mountain
The road was pure ice for over ten miles.
Stop or go slow; don't brake; if you're lucky you keep going.
Sometimes I've gotten drowsy with the sun pouring in;
Pull over, don't drive, sleep, or get some caffeine.
I seldom remember getting tired of driving,
But one morning near Nashville from California,
I feared dozing off and my face started slapping;
But someone took over and I started napping.

Until my thirties I didn't drive far alone;
Now I can hardly believe the places I've gone.
I once flew from Atlanta to Boston and rented a car;
Saw Boston Common, Harvard, the Charles, the Cheers bar;
The Kennedy Library, Plymouth Rock, and Cape Cod.
Drove through New England and on to Ottawa;
Farm land and silos; why did I turn around?

I didn't see enough of the capital town;
And I might have caught a glimpse of young Justin.
Montreal at rush hour; I didn't feel intimidation
To be driving with French signs in an unfamiliar nation;
On to Quebec City, looking for Napoleon's from my car;
Couldn't find it 'til someone told me it was Bonaparte's.

I just remembered back when I dyed my hair blonde,
Men started to wave at me, even a highway patrolman.
When I was forty-eight and still looking young,
And I was wearing my hair long and blonde;
I got involved with a thirty-two-year-old Italian-American;
His few books were about dogs, parrots, and wine;
Told me he loved me, this love-making machine.
He'd more likely watch cartoons and me CNN;
With little in common, what was I thinking?
I was dating him during the Atlanta Olympics,
When, surprisingly, not a problem driving in the traffic.
Rich Blood let me drive his red Corvette
Once, but never again; I don't regret.
He loved his Corvette more than he loved me.
A little bird told me he was seeing his former fiancee;
His parrot, an African grey, said her name, you see;
And she was there when I went to his house one day.
Being with him was worse than being alone;
When driving with him I heard "The Danger Zone."

I drove from Dalton, Georgia, spent the night in Texas, in Dallas;
Then on to El Paso, where I'd live a year;
Then back to Nashville for the night and on past Asheville;
Lucky again, with no breakdowns and little fear.
I liked the climate out West more than I dreamed,
And thought I'd really miss more seeing trees.
Wish I'd gone to Roswell; saw Carlsbad and Santa Fe;
But driving back East, glad to see trees in Tennessee.
I drove one trip from El Paso over to Tucson;
Saw lots of desert, the OK Corral and Tombstone;
Through the Painted Desert going north through Arizona;
Toured the Biosphere and on to the Grand Canyon;

189

I laughed with delight it was so thrilling.
In the Navajo nation I bought turquoise earrings;
Might have been made in Japan or by Chinese.
Many sites on that trip left me in awe;
Like Lake Powell and other sites in Utah.

For part of 2003 I drove to Juarez in Mexico
With a married Muslim couple from Pakistan;
I told them "I'm not a very adventurous woman,"
Oddly, while crossing the border from El Paso.
We were going to a hospital for our clinical rotations,
Right before Mexico was a more dangerous nation.
Soon there would be an awful drug war,
And I'd no longer drive to Juarez in my car.
Juarez was not that safe when I was there;
Many women disappeared; found victims of murder;
And I suspect that twice at the border
Someone slashed one of the tires on my car.
Could it have been the apparently paralyzed beggar?
Haunting me, sliding on his belly, a border regular.
Good doctors in Juarez not wealthy, not even surgeons;
Beggars would ask you for your napkins at burrito stands;
And hospitals kept toilet paper at the nurses' stations.
I was never stopped crossing the border into Mexico,
No surprise, it was harder to get back to El Paso.
My car trunk was often checked by border patrol;
But the couple and I were seldom asked for a passport.
Under an hour to go from Mexico to Texas to New Mexico;
Which I drove about once a month, come rain or shine.
Trust me, rain and snow weren't a problem;
I hate driving in both, but little there of either of them.

I drove from Atlanta through the Everglades,
And I even visited some Seminoles one day.
Didn't notice any alligators, crocodiles, jaguars, or snakes;
Went to Cumberland Island and Epcot along the way;
Saw horses running free on the island; the Atlantic ocean;
Saw Back to the Future at Epcot; never drove a DeLorean;
In Europe at Epcot I saw Paris, France in Florida;
Drove on down to Key West, ninety miles from Cuba.

190

Not to forget I lived in Montgomery;
Right there near the Capital saw the church of Rev King Jr;
And saw the car of Hank Jr and the grave of Hank Sr.
I'd drive from Montgomery seven hours one way monthly.
When I'd drive through Atlanta it always felt exciting;
Maybe feeling something like race car driving.
Once I drove from Montgomery to Mississippi,
And once I drove to New Orleans and Panama City.
I've driven up much of the East coast, a far reach;
I've seen Miami and Myrtle and many a beach..
When I lived in Atlanta I drove all around;
Downtown to work, to shop, in and out of town;
Always exciting; sometimes stuck in a traffic jam.
I thought of King's speech when I often went to Stone Mountain,
And saw the laser show ending with Elvis' "American Trilogy";
And, of course, I had to drive to Tupelo, Mississippi
And see the little house of Elvis' birth I couldn't miss;
And see Graceland, his jets and cars in Memphis, Tennessee;
And at Ole Miss attend the First International Conference on Elvis.

One time I foolishly stopped for a hitch hiker;
Sometimes a woman can be too liberal;
If anything, I wasn't enough fearful;
When I partially rolled down my car window;
I looked at him and reconsidered;
He could have been safe or a serial killer.

I drove to the old Cherokee capital in New Echota;
And saw where the Indians used to live
Before they left on the Trail of Tears.
I drove to Chattanooga and Chickamauga
Where I thought I'd die on the battlefield;
Lightning all around, I, too, felt fear.
I went to Cherokee and saw that Indian nation
And how they live on the reservation.

Once I moved from Atlanta to Cincinnati;
Towed my car behind the moving truck I was driving;

My mind on something else, my heart was breaking;
I had a close call and almost hit a truck accidentally.
The last time I left Atlanta I towed my car on I-285 in rain;
Moved my stuff back home. Will I ever move again?
Thought of a Braves player who once was ashamed
   When he missed the Turner Field exit,
   Went around again, and missed a game.
Once I saw a woman out of her car on I-285;
On that wild road she was lucky to be alive.
Once a patrolman motioned me over
For going too slow but faster than sixty-five.

One week after Christmas I drove to far-off Connecticut
From North Carolina to work at a hospital Yale connected..
For the first time in years saw a cousin in New Jersey;
Her husband a Vietnam Marine vet, heading the war dog memorial;
He an Italian, she now a Catholic and a conservative;
   In their town I saw a place somewhat historical;
   Where Ulysses S Grant had lived, a surprise to me;
Yep, this was far from home near (fictional) Mayberry.
Saw the Liberty Bell and visited my nephew's home near Philly.
Loved it when a tour guide said at Independence Hall
That we only had one king, the King of Rock and Roll.
I didn't have the nerve to drive in New York City,
   But took a tour and saw the Statue of Liberty.
I drove from Pennsylvania across the Alleghenies
   Partly in a blizzard into West Virginia.
   At least it wasn't icy, but I couldn't see
When a truck zoomed by and blew snow at me.
   I pulled over quickly that snowy day,
   And a trucker pulled over quite-a-way away;
And that hero walked back to see if I was OK.
With my winter driving I've had lots of luck,
   But a few times I've been stuck at work.
More than one night on a patient bed I'd sleep,
Afraid to drive home, when the snow was too deep.
   And once after vacation in sunny St John,
   There was a blizzard when I got off the plane.
It looked too dangerous for me to take my home exit,

So I drove to the office at Duke in Durham,
And it's a good thing I didn't go home,
For I needed to be there since some couldn't make it.

Which brings me to my last trip, to Washington DC,
Where I've always found new sites to see.
I saw blooming tulips and cherry trees;
Pandas at the zoo, museums and Capitol tours;
Beautiful monuments and Union Station still excite me.
Drove from DC and Arlington down to Mount Vernon;
Then on to West Virginia, a pleasant ride.
We stood in Harper's Ferry, a rare place indeed;
It's a small town but with a big history,
Where you can view Virginia and Maryland
If you look across the water on the other side,
Where the Potomac and Shenandoah rivers collide.

The next day down to Raleigh and Highway 64,
One of my favorite highways in the world;
Not that I've traveled most highways on Earth,
But it was the longest highway in my State at my birth;
It goes from coastal North Carolina, you see,
All the way west to Tennessee.
I often drive to Raleigh tho' it's not to work in government;
Although it seems to me it could use some improvement.
(That's why I'm running for the NC Senate.)

For nine years I drove from Stone Mountain
To my Emory job at Grady in Atlanta's downtown;
Or sometimes to the bus or to the train station;
To the fifth busiest public hospital in the nation.
One time I left a TV in my back seat;
Didn't lock my door, I would forget;
Don't think I ever forgot again;
But my TV wasn't stolen and no one broke in.
One night about nine my car wasn't there
Where I parked it that morning. What a scare!
For a few minutes no one was around;
Then I walked into a building and here's what I found:

My car had been towed ten miles to a new location;
Luckily, an Emory bigwig came along and took action;
Took me to my car and to an ATM machine;
I'd never park in a wrong spot again.
Turns out he's the one who signed my payroll check;
I must admit, I've had some luck.

So, my car and I are now back home,
About a mile from where I was born.
I've been other places at home and abroad
And have no idea where else I'll hit the road.
It may be near; it may be far,
But I'm sure I'll enjoy driving in my car.

It's Not Mayberry

When I moved to Montgomery and became part of a bunch
Who worked in an office where some went home for lunch;
It just so happened that three of them were big fans
Of watching at lunchtime Andy Griffith Show reruns;
And since I was from a North Carolina mountain town,
They asked me if it was anything like Mayberry in my hometown.
I answered, "No, it's more like Peyton Place";
For I think it's always had a high divorce rate.

Where one's second ex-wife may be dating one's
first ex-wife's third ex-husband;
Where one stops seeing again the mother of his child he never married;
Where more than one wife at his weddings his child she carried.
Could he start wearing again his third wedding band,
Since he's started seeing his third ex-wife
In this small-town, but not Mayberry, life?

Where most preachers (and some few priests)
won't perform the marriage service
If the couple is same-sex or the bride or groom has had a divorce;
But where one may just go get an actor for the pretense;
Though not a real preacher; think of the wedding expense
Of the pretty church wedding, the pregnant bride in white;
Her first wedding, with her two children by her side.
And whether the marriage was legal or not,
Who knows if they really tied the knot?

I didn't tell my co-workers about how one Halloween
We couldn't wear masks after the murder of an old woman.
Or the Halloween another old woman invited children.
They thought she might dress up as a witch,
But when she opened the door wasn't wearing a stitch.

195

When I moved to Cincinnati I got a little nonplussed.
Teased about my Southern accent and even asked
If our men were like those in Deliverance.
That was going too far; I took offense.
I didn't mention the Boy Scout leader in my hometown
Who befriended two young teen boys who went missing.
Turns out it was worse than in Deliverance.
He was also a deputy sheriff and who would suspect him?
But he was the one who killed and buried them.
I must add that he wasn't from around here;
As if that should make any difference.
I didn't mention the music minister back at First Baptist Church,
Who was charged with molesting at least one boy in the chorus.
And I didn't yet know about the boy (no kin)
Who told how his uncle would be molesting him
While "Rhinestone Cowboy" played in the background.
Or the step-father sentenced to sixty years in prison
After videos made of him with his child and step-children;
It's nothing like Andy and Barney's Mayberry jail.
Will he and their mother (in prison) who helped go to Hell?
Yet, we hear very little about such crime;
I suspect many are getting away with them.

I didn't tell them about the young man
Who moved to the house beside where my mother was born;
Where he strangled and killed his ex-girlfriend.
The reason he gave was that she got an abortion;
Don't remember a reason he gave for killing a teen;
Before burying her near a bubbling stream.
The local TV news suggested he did more killing;
But after he got lawyered didn't hear another thing
About the other killings that might have been.

A girl hadn't yet married her bad step-brother;
They were about fourteen when they met each other.
What in the world were their parents thinking?
When they let them share a room they were surely drinking.
She was married and a mother before she was sixteen.
A cousin said "That's the most redneck thing I've ever seen."

I don't know much about my hometown sheriffs,
But I don't think we had any Andy Griffiths
Or Andy Taylors or Barney Fifes;
But we had deputies and cops who cheated on wives.
One who took his girlfriend to get an abortion
Said the father of the fetus was a married lawyer.
That's not to say the real ones don't deserve credit;
Many are good and upstanding, of course; I mean it.
Responding first to danger when it's scariest;
And dealing with those such as the young man
Who, believe it or not, in my hometown
Was held not long ago for his plan to join ISIS;
And for killing his neighbor he was arrested.

We had two handsome Eddies, cops at the same time;
One looked like Magnum PI and drove a Trans Am.
One of them caught a pervert who lives too close,
Rubbing himself in a store against women's underclothes;
He also smeared something sticky and icky on groceries.
Mayberry had its characters, maybe a few like ours;
Ernest T Bass was trouble; Otis drank too much;
Mayberry had the good, the bad, the between and such;
But none we watched in Mayberry did as much harm
As the Ernest who killed the girl my brother took to the prom;
Or the girl with her boyfriend involved in killing and burning her mom.

Recently in the news a local man was caught
After killing a man and stealing his truck.
He had partly painted the man's white truck black;
Had initiative and creativity but conscience he lacked.
And a man was spotted drinking a beer and driving a moped while drunk.
If he didn't recycle that can or beer bottle I hope he got sprayed by a skunk.
The thefts the newspaper reports are an interesting sort:
Last week a Bible (no kidding), a helmet, a mower, a car,
And always a variety of thefts from Walmart.
Frequent arrests for methamphetamine,
And hard to believe all the awful heroin.
While many in courtrooms their freedoms lose,
A judge may take home for himself confiscated booze.

At least that was the rumor years ago,
Where voting holy rollers kept alcohol illegal at the poll;
Still, a high schooler driving a school bus got a DUI,
And so did a fourteen year old, my oh my.
And at least a couple of teens had sex on a school bus;
Nope, it's not Mayberry to many of us.

Sure, there's good and there's bad wherever you go;
And although it's not Mayberry, it may be better than most.
But we all feel better watching The Andy Griffith Show;
And after writing this I need a double dose.
That was going to be the end, but I have to add
How proud I am of Opie, that young lad.
Among a great cast none more awesome;
And so proud of the man he's become.
(I just watched his series on Albert Einstein.)
Proud of The Andy Griffith Show we had;
That we can watch those reruns I'm so glad;
In a world where we see way too much bad.
We can watch those reruns now with children;
Glad to carry on the good lessons they learn.

Lewis and Scott

Let me tell you about my two favorites
Of all the newspaper humor columnists.
They are Scott Hollifield and Lewis Grizzard;
Lewis died, but Scott lives not far from my yard.

Lewis Grizzard's many book titles tell a lot alone:
"If I Ever Get Back to Georgia, I'm Gonna Nail My Feet to the Ground";
About how unhappy he was writing for a newspaper in Chicago;
"If Love Were Oil, I'd Be a Quart Low";
"Don't Sit Under the Grits Tree with Anyone Else But Me";
A clue to how Southern he would always be.
(And, saying that, Lewis was not always PC)
"My Daddy Was a Pistol and I'm a Son of a Gun";
"Don't Forget to Call Your Momma; I Wish I Could Call Mine";
"Elvis is Dead and I Don't Feel So Good Myself";
A reminder and foreboding of how too soon both left.
Many more books plus four newspaper columns a week;
Sometimes on "Designing Women" and invitations to speak.
He loved the Georgia Dawgs and Atlanta Braves baseball,
Whether they were winning or not winning at all
I heard he told about when an actual bulldog, Uga
Came on the Georgia field licking a certain part;
"I wish I could do that," said a good ole Georgia boy;
Whose buddy said, "Uga would bite you if you did that!"
Wrote about Hank Aaron beating Babe Ruth's record home run;
Seems he wrote about the Ted Turner and Tug McGraw race
for fun;
When each pushed a baseball with their noses around the bases;
Later the Braves went from worst to first in the World Series!

I no longer live in Atlanta and Lewis is gone,
But Scott helps make my hometown a better home.
I love how Scott Hollifield can often be ridiculous,

Helping lighten our lives and not be so serious.
He manages somehow to make Kim Jong-un
Seem less worrisome, making the news more fun.
Once when I read in the local newspaper
That someone had stolen Scott's mother's Geo Tracker,
I thought, "I can't wait to see what he writes about that";
Sure enough, he wrote about it and didn't disappoint;
Nor when the newspaper was bought by Warren Buffet;
Not that Mr Buffet our hometown newspaper will visit;
But if Mr Buffet did from the front door he'd see
Where Scott's wife works at the public library;
And Scott's mother's home just up the street.

Sometimes I wonder how I got so lucky
As to live when these writers make life less yucky.
Scott makes it easier to not miss Lewis;
Sometimes, Scott, too, even writes about Elvis.
The genius of these two funny, witty writers
Is that Scott makes life in a small town seem part of something bigger;
And Lewis made life in a big town seem part of something smaller;
And feeling like you're part of something good really matters.

Basketball

Last night perhaps the best team ever,
The Warriors with Durant and Curry,
Beat the Cavaliers with King James;
He was awesome, no reason for shame.
Love watching these teams,
A ball lover's dream;
Durant, Curry, James, all the others;
NBA champions, basketball brothers.

Not hard to see they're mostly black;
It wasn't that way not so many years back.
Hard to imagine before integration
All the missed opportunities due to segregation.
When I was a girl in our less great America and world,
Few blacks on college teams; some were pro;
Not just the Harlem Globetrotters who started in Chicago;
Man, could those Globetrotters put on a great show;
Great Globetrotters like Curly and Meadowlark Lemon,
Goose, Geese, Tex, others, Wilt the Stilt Chamberlain.

After high schools merged and one was bigger,
We saw more than one great high school player;
When our local high school played their teams;
Maybe more than our fair share, it seems;
Who went on to be taller and even greater;
Like seven feet four TALL Tommy Burleson;
James Worthy, Sleepy Floyd, and David Thompson
(his school nearby, not sure if his played ours);
Their teams national championships won.
Thompson led NC State to beat the UCLA Bruins
UCLA had been seven-year straight national champions.

I'm a fan and native of North Carolina
From way back, with teams no finer.
Coach Dean with our own Worthy and Jordan;
Hometown Roy's team again won the final.
And who could forget NC State's Jimmy V
Running down the court in victory?
His "Never give up!" still means a lot;
You had to cheer his soul, his heart.
I've even pulled for Duke, with Coach K.
I pull for all the ACC, I guess I'd say.
And Dream Team or not, for the USA.

I loved basketball since I was four;
I remember my sister out on the floor;
Her team won the tournament in '52.
My other sister in her seventies still plays, too.
My brother won a game with a shot from afar;
Had cousins who were high school stars;
One was the county's basketball MVP;
I was sad I didn't get to go and see.
Another I think had our highest school score,
When one game he made forty-four from the floor.

Made my first goal from an old barrel ring
I hung on the wood shed, proud of that thing.
Later Daddy put up a better ball goal;
Ten feet high (me five feet), just like a pro.
In sixth grade was my day of fame;
I scored thirteen against seventh grade in a game;
Hit seven of eight, missed second free throw;
Seems I could hardly miss the goal.
At home after school looking forward to the day
When on the high school team I'd play.
I'd shoot many baskets, a hundred or two;
Oh, how I loved it; I still do.

But then I became self conscious and short,
And a part of me gave up the sport.
Some in the family said I was too skinny;

Even the coach said I was puny.
Don't pay attention to some who would say
Bad things to hurt you, to get in your way.
Set good goals; don't dare to dream;
Remember "Never give up!" if you might make the team.
(Note: Michael Jordan as a teen didn't make a high school team;
And Stephen Curry didn't make a major college team;
And we all know they went on to far exceed any early dream.)

Coach Dean Smith

—⊸⊙⟡⊙⊶—

Coach Smith means more to North Carolina than basketball;
Much more than being one of the winningest coaches of all;
Beloved by his players, like a second father;
And not just to ones like Jordan who are greater;
But to some who never became an NBA star.
Some said he was the best basketball teacher;
(And Michael Jordan his best basketball learner).
Coach Smith was against war, for civil rights and justice;
His father had integrated his high school team in the '30s in Kansas.
Coach Dean would integrate places in the '50s;
He gave Charlie Scott a scholarship in the '60s;
One of the first black athletes at a major southern school.
It might seem that integration was helping the African-American;
But, in fact, it was best for all our countrymen and women;
No real reason to give anyone credit for just doing the right thing;
(Still impressed player Sam Perkins helping in South Sudan).
African-Americans have made much money for universities;
Not getting paid but bringing in billions with their victories;
And this is something I'm sure Coach Smith knew.
The victory I cheered the hardest and remember the most
Was when North Carolina beat Georgetown in 1982.
Freshman Jordan made that last great shot and Georgetown lost.
I remember our states' natives; some played against our local high school;
Like James Worthy, the tournament's Most Outstanding Player.
Georgetown had Patrick Ewing and NC native Sleepy Floyd.
Georgetown's coach John Thompson was a worthy opponent;
In the '76 Olympics he had been Coach Smith's assistant;
And, supposedly, Coach Smith had helped him get his job at Georgetown;
Of course, Coach Thompson was capable and
might have gotten it on his own;
For Thompson became the first coach who was African-American
To win a major college sports championship in our nation.
To both coaches it is a great testament

That when Coach Smith died, John Thompson said, "I love him."
Another story I found quite touching but about more than basketball
Was when the Yankees asked a New York boy to pitch the first baseball;
But dying Jimmy V was too sick to go to Yankee stadium,
And Coach Dean Smith filled in for him.
Coach Roy Williams was Smith's assistant for ten years,
And has often spoken how Coach Smith he reveres.
Michael Jordan and many players at Coach Smith's memorial
At Chapel Hill; their second father, their second home;
Where else but the Dean Smith Center, the Dean Dome?
Many remembering him in and out of the gym;
Many others, too, will long respect and revere him.

Wikipedia a source, obtained August 20, 2017

Coach Jim Valvano

The wins I remember the most were in 1982 and 1983,
When North Carolina, then NC State had a national victory.
You can read my poem about Coach Smith at UNC,
But NC State's Coach Valvano is also legendary.
His 1983 basketball team was called "the Cardiac Kids";
They'd come so close we'd nearly flip our lids;
Excitement from Coach V and the team we didn't lack;
It's a wonder they or we didn't have a heart attack;
Like when the score was tied and at the last second,
Lorenzo Charles dunked an alley-oop thirty-foot ball
Dereck Whittenburg threw, for NC State to take it all.
When they won the national championship who can forget
How Coach Valvano ran up and down the court?
I remember Houston they beat had great Olajuwan;
Virginia had already lost with great Ralph Sampson.

Coach Jimmy V would coach for seven more years;
For three he was also NC State's Athletic Director in his 30s;
And in 1989 named ACC Coach of the Year;
He was having an amazing career.
Better than some of his players were doing in classes;
And you know about those college sports controversies;
Not all college players can be passing students;
And even though their talents are bringing in millions;
And even though they weren't getting paid for their talents;
And even though they're working hard and learning life lessons;
College sports has some tough standards.
The wasted year of calculus I never used counts,
Like some art and ancient history and subjects of all sorts;
Coach V was put on sports probation and under pressure resigned.

He would go on to be an ESPN and ABC sports announcer;
About ten years later Coach Valvano had cancer.

He traveled and continued to be a motivational speaker.
He spoke at the ESPYs accepting the Arthur Ashe Courage Award,
Saying "Never give up!" He died in 1993 at age 47 eight weeks later.
He's known also for other things he would say;
Like "If you laugh, you think, you cry, that's a full day";
Like "Cancer cannot touch my mind...my heart...my soul."
Some say, "When God made Jimmy V, he threw away the mold."

I was thrilled to discover that my grand-daughter's teacher
Was Coach Jimmy V's daughter Jamie who traveled with him
When he was speaking and inspiring while dying with cancer;
And she was at his famous speech at the ESPYs with other family.
His 1983 team didn't get to go meet with the President
Until Jamie went with them more than thirty years later to meet Obama.
It was sad that Lorenzo Charles couldn't be with them;
He had died at age 47 in 2011 in Raleigh in a vehicle accident.
I asked my grand-daughter if Ms Valvano was back at school;
She said, "Yes, she was, and the two of us were sweeping;
Ms Valvano said, 'One day in the White House meeting with the President;
The next day back at school sweeping the lunchroom."
My grand-daughter and many of you might not see
Why basketball means so much to me;
And some might think, "Oh, good Lord!"
When I say a great coach is something of a god.

The V Foundation has raised many millions
For treating and researching cancer
At places like Duke where Jimmy V died;
Where there's the Jim Valvano Day Hospital
At Duke Children's Hospital, named in his honor;
Yes, at Duke, an NC State rival,
Another great testament to rising higher.
He was New York bred and finished college in New Jersey,
But his home came to be in North Carolina.
He got too sick to throw out the first baseball at Yankee stadium;
His funeral was on the NC State campus at Reynolds Coliseum;
A large crowd there with lots of love for him.
He's buried in Raleigh twenty spaces from Lorenzo Charles,
And there's still controversy and many quarrels

About what to do about players making the grade;
Not giving them credit when they haven't been paid.
All those great players have raised many millions
For many universities and many of their students;
And I don't care what others might be saying;
I say give them credit and let players keep playing.

Wikipedia a source, obtained August 20, 2017

Trevor Noah

A most touching story is Born a Crime I recently read;
The autobiography of The Daily Show's Trevor Noah;
About being born and growing up in South Africa;
Feeling the effects of that country's apartheid;
Separating blacks and whites from 1948 to 1994.
Born in 1984 to black Patricia, mixed Xhosa and Jewish;
Not married to white Robert, mixed German and Swiss;
When it was illegal for his parents to marry or have relations;
His father moved away; his mother was jailed and paid fines.
He mostly lived with his mother and they were very poor;
Several times a week they would enter a church door;
She was very religious and only allowed the preacher station;
When they listened to the radio in their old beat-up Volkswagen.

South Africa something of a melting pot;
Many tribes, territories and countries make up their lot,
And Trevor Noah became a polyglot;
Sotho, Tswana, Tsongo, some German and Spanish;
Afrikaans, Zulu, and English and Xhosa, of course.

When Trevor was about eight his mother married an abuser,
But she still gave birth to a little brother, then another;
So poor they had to eat awful worms; it could hardly get worse;
Sometimes he stayed with his maternal grandmother;
He didn't often see his biological father.
His mother divorced his step-father after four years;
And one would think that might have settled some of her fears.
Trevor's mother became engaged to another thirteen years later;
Her ex-husband, Trevor's step-father, came and shot her.
He shot her in the head and leg and left her for dead;
The bullet missed her brain and came out her nose;
She walks OK now; as I recall that's how the story goes;
She recovered and thanked God she survived.

Trevor was a rising star going higher and higher;
He had great talent and looks and a loving mother;
Did he dare dream when a kid he could go so far?
At eighteen he starred in a South African soap opera.
He co-hosted and hosted several shows and did great comedy tours.
He did well in a dance contest and hosted the
2010 South Africa music awards.

Trevor's step-father threatened Trevor, too, after his mother was shot.
Trevor left South Africa and moved to Los Angeles.
In the United States he was also an incredible success;
He caught the attention of The Daily Show's Jon Stewart,
In 2014 became The Daily Show's international correspondent;
Then in 2015 The Daily Show host when great Jon Stewart left.
Now Trevor Noah as host is doing awesome;
A long way from when his family was so poor;
When he hated he and they had to eat worms;
Now in New York City when he walks in the door,
He's one of those with ten million-dollar homes.
Trevor Noah doesn't tell that; never brags in Born a Crime;
And he also doesn't complain or whine.
He tells very interesting and both sad and funny stories;
Exposing the reader to a wide variety of cultures.
I don't think I've ever read a book more touching.
I'd recommend it on school book lists; it's never boring.

*Reference Trevor Noah's book Born a Crime; also, Trevor Noah Wikipedia, obtained 8/21/2017.

The Saddest Poem in the World

Every year over 200 million pregnancies;
Over 50 million spontaneous abortions;
Over 40 million induced abortions;
Can we, should we save the young ones?
Some say abortion is murder, a sin;
Some say it's better than lives in pain.
If we don't save them, then when abort them?
When are they feeling, hurting humans?

If they are saved and kept alive,
Still 10,000 children under five
In this world die every day;
Is what the world statistics say.
1,000 all ages die each day from malaria;
And nearly a thousand die from hunger;
Twenty million this year may die of famine
In Nigeria, South Sudan, Somalia, Yemen.

Millions others needlessly suffer
With diseases like dementia and cancer.
Some are senselessly kept alive
When they no longer want to survive.

Many innocent languish in prison
Due to injustice for no good reason.
Some have been forced to wrongly confess;
Some the victims of being oppressed.

There may now be 50 million slaves;
Hard to imagine in these modern days;
Condoned by the Bible for centuries
With, "Slaves, obey your masters."
Many are secret slaves kept hidden

Where the truth about them is forbidden;
Many are sex slaves of evil men,
Mostly poor boys and girls and women.

Today more than 60 million refugees,
While many of us ignore their pleas.
Some of us can do more than others
For our fellow humans, sisters and brothers.

Wealth inequality, so much injustice;
Do the rich work more than others of us?
Yet about sixty people have as much wealth
As half the world, many with bad health.
There are mass attacks around the world,
And many of these are not just attacks in wars.
In the United States in the past ten years,
There have been many mass shootings killing at least 10:
32 died in a mass shooting in Virginia in April 2007;
13 in New York in April 2009; 13 in Texas in November 2009;
12 in a Colorado movie theater in July 2012;
27 in Connecticut at Sandy Hook Elementary
School on December 14, 2012,
When a young man shot and killed 20 first graders, 6 adults and himself;
12 in Washington DC September 2013; 14 in California in December 2015;
49 in Florida in June 2016; 59 in Nevada in October 2017;
Many more before and many that killed fewer with shooting;
Like the Columbine, Colorado school shooters who killed 13 in 1999;
And the shooter who shot Congresswoman Giffords and killed 6 in Tucson
In 2009, including a little girl who was born on September 11, 2001;
When about 3000 people died when terrorists attacked the US by plane.

Some work hard to do their part,
To share and help with soul and heart.
We sure can't fix all these things,
But we can try and be better human beings.

Now I'm adding an addendum:
17 killed this week at a school in Florida, again by gun;
And if something's not done, more to come.

Refugees and Royals
Who Cares?

—◦⊙◦—

Queen Elizabeth of England
Married to Philip the Prince;
Then could be Charles the King;
Will Camilla be Queen or Princess?
Who cares?
William and Kate may be nice;
Someday they may be King and Queen;
But what I think is royal vice,
You may think it is I being mean.
Who cares?
Royals should be assigned to the past;
A bad system; it shouldn't last.
Being born doesn't make you more special
Than anyone else, nor should racial.
Who cares?
Being a royal shouldn't get you more
Than someone else born desperate and poor;
Yet we fawn on the royals but ignore the pleas
Of millions of Earth's wars' refugees.
Who cares?

Robots and Hackers

As if there's not enough to worry about
We now have to worry about the robot;
The development of artificial intelligence,
A new and most likely dangerous sense.

When people like Musk and Hawking are warning,
We may want to make robots with caution.
I really hadn't thought of it until last year;
Then on a drive I began to fear.
I was driving to a university to hear Chelsea speak
At a Clinton rally in South Carolina in 2016.
The day before on my home computer,
I RSVP'd and never dreamed that later,
Even though the invitation didn't name the street,
My phone would take me to the building of the meet.
I entered only Main Street, Spartanburg, SC;
Several streets from where the building would be;
On my phone navigator, to the surprise of me,
From my home computer to my phone navigator,
AI took over, whether worse or better.

Human intent isn't always pure,
And with artificial intelligence we can't be sure.
Human hackers are bad enough,
And robot hackers could do bad stuff.
We hear a lot about hackers these days;
So much I know a child in second grade,
When told to write a story like a well-known tale,
Wrote about hackers and The Three Little Viruses.

We hear about the Patriot Act;
Does that mean our government can hack?
Now we have to worry about our own spies;
Hard to figure out the good and bad guys.

How much did Wikileaks hurt or help?
Did hackers use Wikileaks to get people killed?
And did it help to show civilians getting killed?
Seems to me like that should be revealed.
Snowden fled the country; Manning went to jail;
Not sure about Assange; it's hard to tell.
Trump said "I love Wikileaks" for the wrong reason;
Trump's not my favorite human being.

Tesla and others are making driverless cars;
And cars can be controlled by remote radar.
Wonder if Michael Hastings was killed that way,
When his car motor blown over FIFTY YARDS away!

On a lighter note, a reflection of our times,
Hackers put lewd messages on flashing road signs;
But such hacking could become deadly serious,
If hackers put something on the signs really dangerous.

A few months ago my computer was hacked
While on Fox News Facebook I was trolling.
I was locked out; guess my files were stolen;
Thankfully, my important files were backed.
I had to buy a new computer, change passwords and such;
Took a hammer to the old one; glad it wasn't worth much.
Somehow, I think it was not coincident;
That due to my trolling for me it was meant.

And I would be remiss to not mention
The problems with hacking in the last election.
Sometimes it seems there's too much fuss among us
About whether or not we should blame Russia.
But one thing's for sure, a well-known fact;
It will only get worse if we don't act.

Do I sound paranoid? You damned right I am;
And you should be too; there's too much scam.
When Musk and Hawking and others smarter than me
Can't even imagine all the possibility.

Don't get me wrong, I'm all for progress,
But I also know it can become a mess.
Machines for sure can make life better,
Or take jobs away from many a worker.
Will robots go to war? We already have drones.
There are so many unanswered questions.
When possibility becomes reality,
Will good rule over evil? That concerns me.

Hypocrisy

Something that really bothers me
Is all the religious hypocrisy;
Like it's a sin to be LGBT;
But what about all the adultery?
King Solomon known to be good and wise,
But he had 300 concubines and 700 wives.
King David wrote those worshipful psalms,
But sent Bathsheba's husband to the front lines;
Sent Uriah away to war to die
So David with Bathsheba could lie.
Many Mormons and Muslims have had multiple wives
All at the same time; it's polygamy.
Seems something like adultery to me;
Yet many found nothing wrong with their lives.
And what about those who are divorced?
Those who remarry; should they feel remorse?
And what about those who lie and cheat?
Who is better and who is worse?
The divorced, the liar, the cheater, the LGBT?
I've seen a church sign say "REPENT OR BURN!"
Maybe that helps some from sin to turn.
But are you sorry you're not with your ex-husband or wife?
Are you really sorry you now have a better life?

Another disgrace is the treatment of women
And the hypocrisy in saying they are sinning.
You'll even find it in 14:34&35 of I. Corinthians,
How in the church they should keep silence;
And if they learn they'll ask their husbands;
Still ignorantly used by some even today
To say a woman should not be president of the USA!
The Koran says women are a pollution;
Yet several women may have the same husband;

And in many places religion is the reason
There is suppression of women and other suffering.

Hypocrites have wrongly used religion
To justify when they want to be mean;
Even those whose religion is Islam or Christian;
Some used Colossians 3:22, and Ephesians 6:5
To keep millennia of wrong slavery alive.
Even today there are many slaves of men:
Sex slaves--boys and many girls and women.

Some so-called Christians used to burn others at stakes,
Because others didn't believe in talking snakes.
Or was it for denying trans-substantiation during mass,
That the wine becomes the blood, the bread the body of Christ?
Seems Catholics even burned Oxford and Cambridge scholars,
According to Foxe's Little Book of Martyrs.
The stakes called "faggots"; now a slur for LGBTs;
Seems they burned them, too; such hypocrisy.
And what about all the killing in old and new crusades?
Terror, War on Terror, the mujahideen these days?
I heard a Holy Roller recently say she believed
That the 20th century Holocaust in Germany
Was justified because the Jews killed Jesus;
Because the Bible says generations shall die.
"That is just evil!" I want to shout and cry.
What about "Thou shalt not kill?"
Some will answer, "For it's God's will."
Yes, some even justify evil using the Bible,
And believe such stories as the Great Flood and Babel;
Two of all land animals got on Noah's big boat,
And for forty days and nights on water did float;
Prey and predator, but a lion didn't eat a goat.
As for Babel, I don't think languages happened like that.
And the Bible has many a contradiction;
The worst to me the crucifixion.
God gave his son for the Jews to kill?
Sounds too much like an ancient pagan ritual.
And I say if you claim to be a Christian

And want to see Christ kept in Christmas;
How about keeping Christ in Christian?

The Koran clearly condemns all infidels;
Says if you don't fight them you'll burn in Hell;
Says cut off their fingertips and cut off their heads.
Is that truly the teaching of Muhammad's?
"Infidels are your enemies; they deserve torture;
They deserve burning in Hell as their forever future."
The Muslims are not alone with Hell fire;
I've heard Christian preachers give warnings so dire;
Say, "All non-Christians and homosexuals should burn in Hell!"
Good God! What about judge not, pray tell?
What about the Golden Rule? Thou shalt not kill?
What about the suffering people feel?

And, also, according to the Koran,
With many rules for woman and man;
Muslims are not to divide into sects.
Does that mean many Muslims are hypocrites?
And I know among Christians, there are many hypocrites, too;
But I'm pretty sure Jesus wouldn't say, "Kill the Muslim or Jew."
And whether Jesus was supernatural or not;
And whether or not he was really a prophet;
And whether or not he could perform a miracle;
I prefer a prophet who doesn't strike terror.

I think it's evil to say non-believers and homosexuals
Should be tortured, killed or beheaded or burn in Hell.
They may be as good as anyone, truth to tell.
Who will be next? Scientists and intellectuals?
And although we have "judge not" and the Golden Rule:
"Do unto others as you'd have them do unto you";
Hypocrites who are certainly no better
Use religion to justify slavery, racism and bigotry;
The bad treatment of LGBTs and women;
Infidels and many others of their fellow humans.

I understand religion can serve a good purpose;

Can bring comfort and hope and help many among us;
But we need to think of our hypocrisy
And how better all of us people can be.
Don't use your religion to justify evil;
Don't be a big hypocrite; don't be a devil.
And whether there is or is not a God,
Like the Humanists, I believe in good.

Our Beautiful Earth

From sunrise to sunset, from sea to sea;
Mountaintops to ocean depths, so much beauty;
First frost in fall, fresh snowfall in winter,
Buds blooming in spring, crops in the summer.

The underwater world, waves hitting beaches,
Peaceful ponds, lazy and raging rivers,
Waterfalls and rapids, great lakes and small,
Oases, oceans, islands; a reason for them all?

Prey and predator, fishers and fishes;
Inhale, exhale, fed and food, photosynthesis;
Renewables and others, ores and resources;
Even porcupines and porpoises have purposes.

Butterflies and birds or beasts of burden;
Babies and children, animal and human;
Adults; dawn to dusk, dusk to dawn;
All are precious like the spotted fawn.

Atolls, alpine forests, snowy mountains, melting glaciers,
Volcanoes, caves, creeks, crevasses, craters;
The underworld, above, the deep earth's layers;
Seven continents, seven seas, and more than seven wonders.

Sparse and thick shrubs, cacti and cattails,
Flowers and seaweed, savannas, plateaus,
Jungles and tundras, hills, plains, and coasts,
Marshes and mesas, trails and tropical forests.

Gray rocks, green moss, red clay and dirt and red algae;
Blue-green seas, tall redwoods, the giant sequoia;
Green leaves and pine needles on trees big and small;
Beautiful colorful leaves in the fall.

Roads, bridges, buildings, dams, and tunnels;
The Autobahn, the Chunnel, many a highway;
The Great Wall, the pyramids and other wonders;
Our Swannanoa Tunnel and Blue Ridge Parkway.

Calm winds and fierce, lightning and thunder;
Downpours and droughts, afternoon showers;
Gray and black skies when storm clouds gather;
Blue skies and cloud shapes, all kinds of weather.

Roses are pretty and I know I've been rosy;
And haven't mentioned the rows that need hoeing;
Or the weeds that need pulling or the grass that needs mowing;
Or the things that need power or the boats that need rowing.

Difficulties, disease, drought, dastardly deeds, wars to fight;
Drownings, disasters, measles and malaria, the bad termite;
Staph, strep, spiders, snakes and sharks that bite;
Bears, bees, lions, man and others cause great fright.

Buildings, fashions, mansions, monuments, malls;
Tents, stores, stations, stadiums, arenas, great halls;
Schools and jails, homes and homeless, some humble abodes;
Hospitals, hotels, condos, prisons, Guantanamos.

Barns and farms, caves, dens, nests and lairs;
Seashells and cells, the bodies of others;
Cat and dog kennels, puppy mills, shelters;
Waiting for milking, for the rider, for slaughter.

An amazing array of plants and creatures;
A world of natural and man-made features;
All colors, all shapes, polluted and pure;
Worth cleaning up, of that I'm sure.

Smoke and smog, blue skies turned gray;
Some waters clean and clear, some muddy and dirty;
A need for action with no more delay;
Time for some to stop being so greedy.

Challenges and pleasures, our very life, too;
Sustenance at risk; I fear it's true;
A world of wonder, all worth saving;
Protecting from pollution, worth appreciating.

The Earth blessed us with the balance of nature;
Earth nurtures us and she we should nurture;
It's not nice to dishonor ones's mother;
For we will never have another.

Twins' Grandmother

I was so eager to be a grandmother,
And more than a little annoying,
When I bought my daughter
Baby clothes before she was even expecting.

Her husband decided he was ready
To stop being as wild and rowdy;
To spend less time with punk rock
And more time at home and with work.
He went from "My Mind's Mine,"
Singing "Old enough to die";
Screaming "Why am I still dry!"
To being a family man.
When they went for the ultrasound
It was twins they found;
Not just twins, two sons;
Around twins our world turns.

I kid you not; due August 16th;
And anyone who knows me
Knows I love Elvis, a twin;
And that is a big anniversary.
And for some strange reason,
Before the pregnancy or the ultrasound,
I said more than once, "You might have twins."

What will we name them?
We like music, the Beatles.
What about John George and Paul Richard?
Of course, I also said Jesse and Elvis.
I could already see them up on a stage;
The newest stars, the latest rage;
Elvis and Jesse reincarnation;

My own and others' fascination.
(Or at least a Presley impersonation)
But their daddy would rule; my names brought frowns;
Since their daddy liked football, the Cleveland Browns;
He picked Dixon and Turner; we like the sounds;
Added good family names, Michael and Franklin.

Joy with worry of what can go wrong,
But my daughter did everything right;
She even stopped smoking, was strong;
For them she would always fight.
My daughter, five-two, became high risk;
She and the twins in danger, on bed rest.
I read and studied, which made it worse;
Sometimes knowing too much can be a curse.
Like Caesar's mother, my daughter was cut;
All else went well, the babies were out;
Five fingers on hands, five toes on feet;
And they weighed about five pounds each.

Two precious bundles, so much love;
Maybe there is a God above.
I never dreamed we would feel all the joys
As we would get from those little boys.

Boy Genius

We knew he was smart,
But little did we know
Into a genius he would grow.
Did I have a part?
I'm a Mensan, borderline, I'm sure;
Bookish and love learning; it's true.
BA, MA, MS, MD, PsyD;
Have studied many an -ology.

Last year in first grade I said to him,
"Your body has an immune system,
And when you are sick with fever
It is fighting viruses or bacteria."
From then on he would surprise us;
He talked about t-cells and other fighters.
When their chihuahua died he said it was "pancreatitis";
When I asked, "What else?" he said, "hemorrhagic gastroenteritis."

He asked if I knew about something called CRISPR;
No, I hadn't yet heard of that technology;
He explained it can cure certain cancers;
Said "There are many types" he would study.
Then second grade and the teacher inquires,
"Who can tell me the three forms of matter?"
He says, "Actually there are five"; the teacher in awe;
"Solids, liquids, gases, Bose-Einstein condensates, and plasma."

I asked him why we don't feel dizzy
Since Earth is spinning around so quickly;
"Why is it that we don't feel it?"
He quickly answered, "classical relativity";
Then showed me a video about it in a minute.
He worships Einstein but was somewhat concerned

That Einstein wasn't admired enough.
I assured him that when I was his age and Einstein died,
Everyone thought he was the smartest person on Earth.
He's wondered, too, how do we know;
If Einstein was right, how do we show?
"Does E really equal m c squared?"
He questioned Einstein; he really dared.
On March 14, he calls, of course,
For pi day is a special day for us;
For it's not just pi to celebrate;
We sing to Einstein, "Happy birthday."

He already knew about Stephen Hawking
When I gave him A Brief History of Time;
(Forgive me if I don't always rhyme)
Before that he was already talking about quantum mechanics,
About entropy and the second law of thermodynamics.
I've read the book twice and still don't understand;
Yet he's eight and he can explain.
Who knows if he knows about what he's said?
For it's over all of the rest of our heads.

I told him about Kary Mullis, from North Carolina;
How he got the Nobel prize for PCR and DNA;
How the Human Genome Project he accelerated;
Suddenly from the boy genius home computer
DNA appeared on TV in another room a little later.

One day it may be anatomy and physiology or hacking;
Tells me why I need to learn computer coding.
The immune system, the heart, the lungs, the brain;
Do you know the amygdala is the center of emotion?
Or why the UK dropped out of the European Union?
Yes, he knows that Brexit is "British exit,"
And, of course he didn't stop at that;
"There's Northern Ireland; no official Southern; it's the Republic of Ireland."

Biology, cellulase, cellulose, other sugars;
Photosynthesis, carbon dioxide, clean air and water;

Pollution, the climate, global warming;
Why are so many people still harming?
Chemistry, chlorophyll, heavy water, deuterium;
Explains why plutonium not an isotope of uranium.
Acids, bases, oxidation-reduction; what about God?
Tells me why Mars is red. Wonders about a lot.
He's also interested in philosophy;
"Do you know about Kantianism?" he once asked me.
I was relieved to think a few seconds and respond,
"You mean the philosophy of Immanuel Kant?"
"Do you want to know why I think utilitarianism is important?"
He asked, not knowing, that before his daddy Jeremy was born,
I kept a utilitarian Jeremy Bentham quote in my wallet.
Psychology, too, behavior therapy;
"It's just classical conditioning."
He's still just eight with such reasoning;
It's all quite amazing to me.

We owe the computer for much that he knows;
All kinds of You Tube and other videos;
A world of knowledge to grow his mind;
Seems he was born at the right place in time.
But he worries about Trump and our country,
Tho' we try not to worry the kids with the news;
But we worry anyway; it's hard to not hear and see
That there are dangerous and awful opposing views.

Our boy genius wants a better world.
Does he, like me, wonder the worth?
Hawking is saying we have a hundred years;
Hawking may be right, stoking our fears.
Will humans move a colony to Mars or the moon?
Is it possible such a thing could happen soon?
Will we find aliens? Will they find us?
Will humans ever go closer to the Sun and Venus?

How far can computers and robots grow?
There's still so much we cannot know.
Will the world get hotter? Is it beyond repair?

228

Can we fix it or not? Are we already there?
How much will waters rise too high?
How many more species and people will die?
Will AIDS and all kinds of cancer be cured?
Will the Earth be destroyed by nuclear?

Will we learn how to get along better?
Will we ever learn to "Love thy neighbor?"
Yes, we can make the world better;
I say, "Make America and the world better than ever."

We wonder what will become of our boy genius,
Our Earth and our children, theirs, and all of us.
Is his future bright or is it dim?
For all of us, for all of them, for him?

Climate Crisis

We live in a world of increasing alarm
That the climate crisis will cause great harm.
We've heard environmentalists long decry,
While others among us strongly deny.
First, Al Gore warned us of global warming;
Said carbon emissions and pollution are harming;
Warned us well before the new millennium;
When there was still time for acts of prevention;
Warned us about it with Earth in the Balance;
Made some progress at the Kyoto Conference;
But some people laughed; there are always naysayers;
President Bush 41 even called Al Gore crazy.
Now 200,000 people die of pollution each year in our country.
We went from global warming to climate change;
Too many typhoons flooding places like the Philippines;
You'd think doubters would believe after Katrina and Sandy;
Houston and beyond hit hard last week by Hurricane Harvey;
This week it's category 5 Irma threatening the East Coast;
The strongest ever, according to scientists;
Two more behind Irma; they've never seen worse;
And severe flooding now in India, Nepal, and Bangladesh.

Out west in several states wildfires are raging;
Not hearing much about it due to all the flooding;
Think most scientists agree it has to do with global warming.
Last fall wildfires killed 14 in nearby Tennessee;
The fires so fast they didn't have time to flee.
Two were girls 9 and 12, who died with their mother;
Survived by their father and 15-year-old brother;
Heard they're offering their home for victims of Harvey.
Rev Dr Ed Taylor was another who died; he was 85.
Some claim he performed about 85,000 marriages,
Including one for Patty Loveless, one for Billy Ray Cyrus;
He'd perform no same-sex marriages as long as he was alive.

Yes, we face a truth inconvenient;
Some choose to ignore for reasons of profit.
It's hard to explain to children who are learning
Why many conservatives don't seem to stand for conserving;
When clean air and water and food need protecting;
When saving the Earth is how we should be progressing.
Al Gore made a film when he lost the presidency;
"An Inconvenient Truth" warned us again of the urgency.
Now icebergs breaking from rising sea to rising sea;
Temperatures rising to a new degree;
From Antarctica to the Arctic, Greenland between.
What about the amber waves of grain, the fruited plain?
The much greater number of earthquakes in Oklahoma?
Fooling ourselves about the effects of fracking;
And what will happen in California, Manhattan and Miami;
Ignoring the obvious when evidence not lacking.

Now we have a climate crisis;
Some choose to ignore the warnings of scientists.
Al Gore and others have made more films,
Yet many still don't listen to them.
And now we have a US administration
That seems unconcerned about our world and our nation
When it comes to the greatest threat we face;
Some give more thought to the get rich race.
When we should be doing more about disease and health,
Too many are trying to get too much wealth.
We have a president who pulled out of the Paris Climate Accords,
Giving reason to add to our already great worries.
We may not see the worst results of our ways,
But our grand-children may see our Earth's last days.

The Great American Eclipse
(and segue)

—◦◦◦◦—

Today was the rare great American solar eclipse.
We can still be amazed; it's on everyone's lips.
It's been 99 years since a totality eclipse crossed the entire USA;
From the Pacific to the Atlantic; Salem Oregon
to Charleston, South Carolina;
We watched from Earth on August 21, 2017; I in the afternoon;
When the view of the Sun was blocked when
our Earth lined up with our moon.
It felt good today to see our country come together,
And we mostly had good viewing summer weather.
We've lately had lots of marches and protests and downright fights;
With many people disagreeing about his or her or others' rights.
Last week a man with a car killed one and injured many during the riots;
The one killed was an activist named Heather Heyer;
Her mother at her funeral said her death will magnify her.
Today on TV we saw a place in Nebraska called Carhenge;
Where people had gathered to watch the eclipse and have fun;
Old cars arranged like Stonehenge by some people on a binge;
Reminded us what it means to be a fun-loving American.

Bonnie Tyler sang her "Total Eclipse of the Heart,"
And at least one baby was named "Eclipse" today.
A couple got married at one total eclipse site;
Who ever gets married on a Monday?
Hope they're not star-crossed lovers like so many;
Hope they're less like Scarlett and Rhett and more like Ashley and Melanie;
Hope she's not like Katharina, the shrew, with Petruchio, the tamer;
Hope they're not like Antony and Cleopatra;
Or like Richard Burton (and others) and Elizabeth Taylor.
Hope they're more like President Ike and Mamie,
less like Ike and Tina Turner;

Or Uncle Ike, shot in the belly by Aunt Mamie, his cousin.
Hope they line up more like Jimmy and Rosalynn;
And Tim and Faith and Nancy and Ronny;
And Grandma and Grandpa and June and Johnny.

Often life and literature are full of star-crossed lovers;
With abusers, users, forbidders, liars, the unaware, blameless or blamers,
The doubters, the dying, survivors, the selfish, shameless or shamers;
Like Romeo and Juliet, George Jones and Tammy Wynette;
Hermia and Lysander, Scarlett and Rhett,
Troilus and Cressida, Venus and Adonis,
Burt and Sally and Loni, Priscilla and Elvis;
Michael, Larry, Rich, John, different men, same names, for me and Liz;
Plus one I'm still longing for "The Stars [to] Line Up"* and never part
Rather than feeling "A Total Eclipse of the Heart."*
We like to read and write poetry and didn't fuss and fight;
I think of him every day and night;
I'd love to have the love, the laughs, the life we found.
I was so happy when he was around.

Many marriages are messy like Hillary's and Bill's;
They're not all rosy, we know, with passion and thrills.
Bill and Hillary, like some, stayed together through it all;
They'd rise again and again together after each fall.
More often, perhaps, there is less forgiving,
And many star-crossed lovers end up divorcing.

I used to wonder that if there's a God above,
"Why didn't each of us get one perfect love?"
Since for life to continue, procreation is a must;
But too seldom the right one to share our lust.
Love and lust pleasures are precious gifts,
Yet so much trouble when causing rifts;
Or when there's longing for them to last,
Or when looking back at a happier past.
When things line up just right it's a rare event;
And we don't have to look to the heavens above
To see that it often seems a less amazing moment;
Especially with people in life and in love.

But, maybe, too, we sometimes don't see
How good things are and how good they can be;
Especially with all the marvels in nature
We can appreciate more and love to nurture.

*Marianne Faithfull's song "The Stars Line Up"; Bonnie Tyler's song "Total Eclipse of the Heart"

Love Me Tender

Please love me tender;
I am your home, your one Earth
Here for you since birth.

Please love me tender—
Your child, father and mother;
Kin (or not), sister, brother.

Please love me tender;
I am your longing lover;
For me no other.

Please love me tender;
Through life, perhaps no other;
All of us suffer.

Peace

Peace a sacrifice.
Is there ever peace in life?
Oh for peace in death.

Author Biography

—◦◦◉◦◦—

Cheryl Swofford was born in western North Carolina and grew up in a copperhead infested mountain "holler" in the 1950s and 1960s. She remembers life without an indoor toilet or electricity at home, with no TV or phone, growing up in the segregated South, hearing preachers shout about Hell, to her dismay. But that doesn't mean she didn't know that Hitler and the Holocaust were awful or care about the deaths of JFK, MLK, and RFK. She was the fifth of six children of Blanche and Hub ("Daddy Drunk with Guns") Swofford. She married at eighteen, had a daughter and a son, divorced at thirty-four, has had several lovers, has never remarried, but still loves Elvis. She is the very proud grandmother of identical twin grandsons, another grandson, and a grand-daughter.

Cheryl has five degrees from five universities. She got fifty dollars from her family for college. She was a classroom teacher for ten years until she attempted suicide while going through a divorce and severe stress over thirty years ago. Despite much heartbreak, she feels fortunate to have had remarkable experiences and survived them all. She is grateful to have had the health and opportunity to start over, go back to school (and get MS, PsyD, MD), to learn and work in the medical field, largely in clinical research, including at Duke and Emory University Medical Centers.

CHERYL'S POEMS is her first book.

Printed in the United States
By Bookmasters